Journey to the Golden City

VICKI BURKE

Journey to the Golden City

Finding the Way Home

Matador
9 Priory Business Park,
Wistow Road, Kibworth Beauchamp,
Leicestershire. LE8 0RX
Tel: 0116 279 2299
Email: books@troubador.co.uk
Web: www.troubador.co.uk/matador
Twitter: @matadorbooks

ISBN 978 1785899 065

British Library Cataloguing in Publication Data.
A catalogue record for this book is available from the British Library.

Printed and bound in the UK by TJ International, Padstow, Cornwall
Typeset in 11pt Aldine401 BT by Troubador Publishing Ltd, Leicester, UK

Matador is an imprint of Troubador Publishing Ltd

To Mark and Connie.

This book comes with a free digital CD download, available
if you visit www.keystothegoldencity.com/download

Activation code: ST4006/fdd

Reviews for *Journey to the Golden City*

Journey to the Golden City is a powerful personal story of one person's lived experience of discovery of both the deeper and transcendent levels of life. With an openness, oftentimes an appropriate scepticism, and a blossoming intuitive intelligence, Vicki proceeds on her journey one step – sometimes many – at a time and connects consistently and evermore deeply with her special talent and purpose as a musician and as 'the healer' musician. On her way she is discovering the universal truths embedded in the astrological paradigm, as they relate to, enhance and enlighten her own individual life, and she recounts her experience with an infectious warmth and enthusiasm for the healing power of connecting with deeper understanding.

Suzi Harvey is co-author with the late Charles Harvey of *Sun Sign, Moon Sign* and *The Principles of Astrology*. She has for many years worked as an astrological consultant, and more recently and now works as a psychoanalytic psychotherapist.

Reading Vicki speaking her truth in this book, the first line of the I Ching hexagram 'Union' springs to mind: 'Fundamental sincerity is the only proper basis for forming relationships. This attitude, symbolised by a full earthen bowl, in which the content is everything and the empty form nothing, shows itself not in clever words, but in the strength of that which lies in the speaker.'

Vicki's golden Leo rising, heart-warming story introduces us, in her own angelic Piscean way, to something very profound and deep that I suspect will become a major player in our future, for who can argue with the healing quality of music?

Vicki believes in peace, health and happiness; this is why Vicki's optimistic enthusiasm and healing music have such charm. Read her story and maybe she will give you the confidence to find your own peace and tell your own story. It seems to me the more stories we can hear, the better we will understand each other, and gaining understanding of all of us in our amazing variety seems to me to be something worth attempting.

Chrissy Philp, author of *The Golden City*, is a master of the I Ching and astrology and holds an MA with the Sophia Centre. She is a philosopher, writer, artist and exponent of wisdom.

Publishing Information

The World Is Sound by Joachim-Ernst Berendt published by Inner Traditions International and Bear & Company, ©1991. All rights reserved.

http://www.Innertraditions.com Reprinted with permission of publisher.

From *The Valkyries*. Reprinted by permission of HarperCollins Publishers Ltd © *(Paulo Coelho) (1995)*

From *A Short History of Nearly Everything*. Published by Doubleday. Reprinted by permission of The Random House Group Ltd

Cover Notes:
Cover Image by Terry Burke
Design by Kevin Clutterbuck
Photography by Mark Brookes

About the Author

Vicki Burke was born in Bristol, England and lives in the Somerset market town, Frome. Her life as a saxophonist and music teacher began to expand in the millennium as she found a new path to walk as a healer. Having added harpist, singer/songwriter, author and playwright to her list of talents, she has arrived at the conclusion that these titles become increasingly irrelevant as they are just some of the many games that we all can play as we grow and become whole.

This book is about her journey so far.

Acknowledgements

There are many people to thank and words really don't say enough, but here goes.

Firstly, a huge thank-you to my family for their lifelong support and love. Andy, my former partner, for being my gift, my mirror and for sharing this most profound journey with me, thank you. Seb, for waking me up, and for your friendship and love. John Wadsworth, thank you for all your gifts and your generosity. Thank you to Chrissy Philp, Chloe Goodchild and to Tareth for your inspiration. Thank you to Mark Brookes, Louise Chalice, Anthony Thorley and Celia Gunn, Johanna van Fessem, Sue Parsons and Susan Kedward, John Akaysar, Emma Collins, Tim and Sophie Knock, Terry Burke for her wonderful artwork, Martin Maudsley, Susan Mears and Nigel Peace and all the other countless people mentioned in this book and those not mentioned who helped me on my path.

Contents

CONTENTS

Chapter 0

In the Beginning... An Introduction

If you are looking for something that you sense is missing in your life then you must know that you are not alone. If you are feeling this, however, you are already on your way to finding it. Often you can be on a journey and not even realise, but as you get closer to your destination, or maybe only when you arrive, you can look back and see the roads that brought you to this juncture. I have spent my whole life walking this road.

In 2008 all the paths I had been travelling on seemed to converge and I realised that all the stories I had collected on my way, although they were my stories, were everyman tales of self-discovery. The universe is made up of wheels within wheels, cycles within cycles, and this book came at the end of one such cycle, mainly out of a need to document and aid my own healing process. In doing so I hope that it might prove a guide for others walking alongside me, as so many books have guided me.

Before I begin, the most important point I would like to make is that everything in this book is based on my personal findings and so this is my truth. For me opinions and truths are subjective. I am not claiming to make statements of fact, just beliefs that have chimed true in my heart for the moment, knowing that even these may well shift in time as I, and we as a culture, grow. Nothing stays still and everything changes; so says the *I Ching,* or the *Book of Changes.* You are about to enter my stream of consciousness and I hope it offers you some interesting signposts.

This book (and CD) is the first of a trilogy. It is my intention to reveal a mechanism that can help us return to a way of living, reconnecting us to many aspects of life that we have lost sight of over the ages. This twelve-step process is not an original idea, but then again nor is anything I am offering here. That is the core of my understanding: that everything we would do well to bring into our lives is not new to us; it is more a case of remembering what we already know and how we used to live.

We are all on a journey to heal ourselves of the wounds we have endured on our way through the cosmos and how we choose to do this is completely up to us. Looking for threads that can be tied together and mirrors that shine reflections of others back at us is something that humans love to do. We see patterns everywhere and they bring such satisfaction that we can all bathe in the contentment that it brings to our lives. It is my desire to reflect some of the joy I have experienced in weaving these connections back to you.

I would like to begin by giving you the backdrop to the events in this book to demonstrate the mechanism that lies at the heart of ourselves and our world. The twelve stories in each chapter are like windows into my life but if you read them out of context, they would seem like random occurrences. I feel it is important to present to you the background to the stories so you can see that everything has meaning, and this runs like a tapestry through all our lives if we take the time to follow it.

I was born a Jew, but my family were atheists, which created the foundations of my childhood and young adulthood. Underlying all this was a quest for a different story, but as none that resonated came my way, at the time, I wasn't even aware that I was searching for anything. People and teachings came in and out of my life and I tried them on like clothes and discarded them soon enough.

It wasn't until I was thirty-two before I would try on a robe that fitted and the epiphany that picked me up and wrapped me up changed the course of my life. Amazing things began to happen and I soon found, together with my new truth, my real vocation. I began to see my life as a three-legged stool. I was always a musician, I began teaching whilst I was still at school and then, at the age of thirty-four, I became a healer. I soon realised, however, that there is no separation between these worlds as music is both a teacher and a healer. As I sought out new, like-minded companions, who taught me how to discover my healing abilities using crystals, Reiki and my voice, it soon became clear that the most important method of healing for me was going to be through my music.

As well as learning to work with energy, like many who take this road, I began to connect with people who were already on this path and who could teach me new ideas and ways of looking at the world. I also began to read avidly, eager to get my hands on as many books as I could to further my knowledge. One such book changed the way I lived day to day. It was Deepak Chopra's *SynchroDestiny*.

Taking this beautiful guidance on board, I became aware of how synchronicity can be the frame on which our life hangs, from the big picture down to the minutiae. It's the breadcrumbs that lead you forward, left by your higher self, enabling you to remember your way home. It's completely up to us as individuals how we view these moments in our lives but the more we take notice of the signs, the more we see and the more fun we can have with it. Or rather, the more fun it has with you, depending on how you view your life. Letting go of my need to control my life enabled my world to expand considerably.

Events transpired, which I hope to reveal through this journey, that led me to a point where I wanted to create my own project based on all that I had learned. Its main purpose was to create a link between all the new teachings I had looked into, from the Hindu chakras to astrology and from the I Ching to the world of vibration. I called it *Keys to the Golden City: A Musical Journey Around the Cosmos*. I had learned that the golden city, a term taken from the Book of Revelations, is not a place we shall arrive at but a state of mind we are to achieve; an understanding of balance and harmony where we will raise our vibration and reach a higher state of being; a dimensional leap. I wanted to use the word 'key' as a play on words, linking my core objective of bringing the power of music to the healing process. I realised that this desire came from a realisation that I was living out the nature of my astrology. I have my sun and four other planets in Pisces, and Pisces, being the last of the twelve signs, brings all the threads together. Here I began my journey from my head back to my heart. This was my soul purpose.

My quest was also to understand the idea that there could be a link and communication between the world of spirituality and the world of science. I had felt for a long time that they told the same story but just in different languages, and that they were just at different places of evolution. With growing excitement, I began to watch science move ever more rapidly toward the ancient spiritual teachings that were becoming part of my new horizon.

I began by creating an image of the journey of all things, coming from source and showing how they come into being as a reflection of themselves. From the atom to a human, from the Earth to a galaxy, each of these beings are universes in their own right and reflect each other, as each holds the wisdom from that first point of singularity, the Big Bang. Just like the baby that is created from the mother's egg which divides again and again so that each cell in our bodies holds the DNA from that original egg and sperm cell, every state is a 'wholeness' in itself, being both apart from and a part of the whole. This universe, which we believe to be 'all that is', contains all these worlds within worlds inside it, like Russian dolls.

Our universe has been put forward by many early scientists and philosophers, right through to those in the modern age, to be dodecahedron in shape, giving us the symbolic 'twelve' everywhere we look.[1] Looking into the concept of the 'twelve' was another journey into new discoveries. There are, of course, important connections between the elements of time; the months in the year and the hours in the day. The image of the clock face, as a musician, connected very strongly to the twelve notes in the chromatic scale, which I was always shown as a cycle, placing the twelve keys around it as a journey of modulation, i.e. a way of travelling through all the keys in a systematic manner.[2] Adding to this the knowledge that there were twelve disciples, twelve tribes of Israel and twelve imams, the symbolism of twelve becomes highly apparent. When this information was put together with the fact that we have twelve pairs of cranial nerves in our brain, six on each side, and that a dodecahedron is the most efficient shape with the highest number of sides that can all touch when packed together in multiples, it becomes harder and harder to view all this as mere coincidence.[3]

It is this metaphorical, twelve-sided universe (in which the astrologers placed each of the archetypes like faces in a window), this 'all that is' that I call 'God' for want of a better word, with the understanding that we are a living cell in the body of this god, each of these worlds having its own inner wisdom as we do.

I like to apply this vision of the universe as a set of

Russian dolls to the concept of time as space and time, scientists are realising, are not divisible. As time doesn't exist, as we can comprehend it, we have calibrated it to handle our dimensional limitations. I like to map our journey against our solar system as I feel each planetary orbit marks out stages in our life like bar lines in music or verses in a song. We have the turn of the Earth, which gives us our day; the moon around the Earth, our month. The Earth takes a year to orbit the sun; Jupiter takes about twelve. There's our twelve again. Saturn takes twenty-nine years, a very important time of change for many, and Uranus takes eighty-four years to orbit the sun. This is the last planetary orbital return we will experience before we reach the extent of the expansion in our journey, at which point the form collapses, we die and return to source. The candle is extinguished, the solar system implodes and so too, eventually, will the universe, back to its point in space and time, ready for rebirth. Breathe in, breathe out.

My project, which has now grown into a performance of harp, song and journeys, maps the single, seasonal, astrological year, alongside A. T. Mann's twelve stages of man[4] and also journeys in my life. With it, I continue the quest for my own truth and I do, at all times, try to make it clear that everything I speak about is my truth, just as I know you will be searching for yours. The further I travel on this journey, the more I have learned that there are many truths. In fact, there are as many as there are people. As we learn to live alongside each other, learning to love and trust each other, I feel there will be room in the world for each individual's truth to have its place.

This book contains just some of my thoughts and synchronistic stories that brought me to this joyous point in my life. Some of it may seem quite unbelievable and I would be in agreement with you, as some of my stories seem pretty 'unbelievable' to me as well. However, I know that I couldn't have made them up, as I have never been that imaginative and what transpired felt more real than anything I have ever experienced.

I would like to invite you just to suspend your disbelief for long enough to read about what I have to say so that I might interest you enough to look for the path to your own golden city. My aim is only to encourage others in their search. Answers of this nature cannot be passed on; they are for each individual to discover for themselves.

If you are already walking your path or just searching for the key to unlock the first door, remember that the more you are open to the possibility and beauty of synchronistic events, the more you will allow them into your life and the more beautiful and meaningful your life can be.

Chapter 1

A Leap of Faith

Elle

She came into my dreams and kindled the spark,
Like a candle in the dark, my eyes were opened.
She painted on my easel, signs of peace and love,
Like a single white dove flying home.

She came into my song and changed the way I wrote,
I found that just one note was all I needed.
She came into my heart and fixed the broken strings,
Like my harp had grown wings and learned to fly.

She came into my life and set my spirit free,
And now that she is me, we are one.
And now that she is me, we are one.

Our journey begins in March with the Spring Equinox and
the birth of the seasonal year. As we look out our windows we
see the buds bursting through after the winter's stillness, care-
free lambs playing in the fields and the sun's rays remind us

what it is to feel warm again. Nature is enticing us to step out-side. With the thrust of spring and the clocks moving forward, we sense that time is speeding up and the year starts passing with an air of excitement and a quickness in its step. This is a time of great change energetically, seasonally and spiritually.

We have now finally reached the end of the seasonal year and the beginning of the new with the coming of spring. The beginning and the end are as one, the *Aum*, the alpha and the omega. With our inner longing for this sense of newness, the spark that is suddenly ignited as the first signs of life light up our days, like the stars in a night sky, the cycles are seamlessly bridged by a sigh of relief that emanates from all our hearts. The journey to come will be about finding links between all things, joining up all the dots. And if we are truly to embrace the idea of this 'web of connected oneness', then surely we shall find the mirrors everywhere and realise that separation is an illusion, not the truth.

Interestingly, for example, the three religions descended from Abraham – Judaism, Islam and Christianity, separated like a broken family – all have major festivals at this time. Each of these festivals involves fasting as a time of slowing down, doing the inner work to come out of the time of darkness and resurrect oneself or be reborn. It is thought that most of the scriptures were 'received' at this time; it is certainly accepted that Moses received the tablets of stone after forty days and nights in the desert. The gifts are great.

After the restrictions that the cold weather has laid upon us, we are now lifted up with the joy of being unburdened by our winter layers. We become like those spring lambs, playing like children as we shake off the feeling of being a whole year older and remember that we are forever souls. There is a great sense of positivity and a desire to flex the muscles of our personal power.

As I look out at my own back garden, I see the shrub

by the patio doors exploding into life with new, bright red shoots and I have a sudden desire to leap into action. As they grow, the leaves gradually change this vibrant colour to a beautiful green, and I somehow instinctively know they will have a story to tell. Enjoying the renewed sense of curiosity and optimism, like a rebirth, can be universally felt, when we choose to step out from our wintery hibernation.

I felt this most profoundly in 2008, when things were changing in ways I had no control over. Sometimes it just seems that life has a plan for us. I did feel fear, as things certainly weren't all looking good, but I was sensing that at last I was strong enough to withstand what lay ahead. I felt like the figurehead of a ship, ready to take whatever battering was to come, or like a child, too inexperienced to know I could be running away.

To ease me in gently, the universe conspired to bring me something that in younger days I might not have been so happy to get involved with, being of a more cynical nature back then. But as we grow we learn, hopefully, to keep our minds open to receiving life's gifts.

I had never dealt much with astrology as it always had a bad press, literally so. Like most people I had looked at the newspaper and magazine horoscopes once in a while, but never took them seriously; these horoscopes have actually contributed powerfully to the ridiculing of astrology, despite the truth being that it is a very intricate science. If we only judge it by one aspect, our sun sign, which is all that the magazine horoscopes offer, it's like trying to cook following a recipe but only using one of the ingredients – and then complaining that it doesn't taste right. I was not prepared for the extreme accuracy with which a properly drawn-up astrological chart could reveal my inner self.

So it was that in early March I was invited to participate in an astrology course by John Wadsworth, whom I had met some time previously. He had involved me in a wonderful project that he helped to organise called Healthy Concerts, which offered musical events in the comfort of one's own home. Initially, he asked me to play the harp in an advertisement he had created for his astrology course. But after our first collaboration the creative sparks started to fly and so he extended the invitation to accompany the meditations in a twelve-month course, the Alchemical Journey, and possibly sing some of the songs I had been writing that suited the energy of each sign.

The first of the twelve weekends was about Aries, the first of the astrological signs, covering the period from the 21st of March to the 21st of April. It is ruled by Ares, or Mars, the Greek God of war, and its most important qualities are a positive, masculine energy and a creative spirit. It is a fire sign and associated with the colour red. This vibrant sign is all about the self jumping in, leaping without looking. This normally wouldn't have been my kind of thing as I can be quite slow to get active, but then we must be willing and able to accept new challenges and the links were already clearly showing themselves.

I was particularly fascinated when, on the last day, we were introduced to a storyteller who was going to help us create our own spontaneous story. I didn't realise at the time how profound this exercise would be, and how life would soon offer me a powerful sign that I was now on the right path. Such signs are all around us if our minds and our eyes are open.

Our storyteller began by telling us one of his own:

A man lives in a village somewhere in Somerset. He has a house with a beautiful garden that has a splendid plum tree in the middle of it. The man, being a generous-hearted soul, leads a good and contented life, tending his garden well and sharing its gifts.

He understands well the workings of nature and lives according to its cycles. He knows when to put the work in and when to accept its generosity, knowing that when the insects have eaten their fill of the plum tree's fruits and he has offered as much as he can to his neighbours, there is always plenty left for him. When he steps into his garden every day it is almost as if the flowers bend towards him in greeting and honour their mutually balanced and harmonious relationship.

One night he is awoken by a dream telling him to go to Bristol Bridge, where he should wait for a sign. He thinks nothing of it and falls back into sleep. The dream wakes him again and the message is clear. After the third awakening he cannot ignore the message anymore and decides to take the long journey to Bristol. Although it takes three days and nights, crossing fields, sleeping under hedges and eating when possible, the journey is a pleasant one. When he arrives he finds a busy market day and the bridge filled with people. He waits all day looking for a sign, though he has no idea what he is actually looking for. When no sign appears, he watches the traders begin to pack up for the day. He decides, with a heavy heart, that it is time to return home. As he is turning to go, one of the last traders to leave approaches him and asks what he has been doing all day. The trader claims to have been watching the man's suspicious loitering; hanging around without buying anything and seeming to have no purpose. So the man tells the trader that he was guided by a dream, which told him to come here and wait for a sign.

The trader laughs out loud and asks him, "What have you wasted your time for? I would never bother chasing around the country on the basis of a stupid dream. I haven't become a successful businessman," he says, patting his large girth, "by following dreams. In fact, I had a dream, just last night, about a beautiful garden in Somerset with a splendid plum tree in the middle of it that has a pot of gold buried beneath it. But of course I would never waste my time chasing such a dream."

Realising he has received his sign, the man wends his way home with a light skip in his step to his plum tree, where he finds his treasure.

This story had been the basis for Paulo Coelho's book *The Alchemist*, which elaborates on the idea of finding our truth and full potential in our own hearts, and how it takes a journey and the return home for us to discover it was there all along. It was told so beautifully, with such vitality and expertise, I was immediately taken with it and realised that we all have a need to discover our own individual stories to bring more awareness into our lives.

I felt the need to pass this story on. The following day I was due to play my harp at a centre for cancer patients, and in the car on the way I began practising the story to tell it to my good friend Seb, because it was she who was responsible for my epiphany, about ten years before, and we always shared stories that we knew the other would enjoy. As I tried to recall all the details, I realised that the residents at the centre would probably love to hear it too, especially as the harp and story-telling go together so well. However, I had never told a story in public in my life.

Having arrived, we all sat down together to eat and to introduce ourselves, and interestingly there were just twelve people at the table. When dessert arrived there were four bowls of fruit – apples, oranges, pears and bananas – and as I love pears I naturally reached for that bowl. However, as it was being passed to me I saw at the bottom a big, red plum. Without thinking I took the plum instead of the pear.

Then the full significance of the single plum began to dawn on me and I realised that I should tell the story. So I quietly told the nurse therapist sitting next to me what I was feeling, but that I felt a little embarrassed. Suddenly I became aware that all conversations had stopped, everyone was listening to me, and agreed that I should tell the story then and there at the table. So with the whole Arian idea of jumping in without thinking making itself painfully clear, I realised that I had no choice but to tell it.

When I arrived at my friend Seb's the next day I recounted the whole story. After a good deal of laughter we found much to reflect on, loving the richness of the events. As I left her flat, I recalled our twenty-year friendship and how, following her explosive breakdown thirteen years ago, we had cut ties for three years.

We met up again just before I turned thirty-three, and my life was changed forever. It was a long night. We talked for six hours, delicately healing the breakdown in our friendship. She began talking about love and light. She explained about the transformative journey she had been on, and how in the new world she inhabited she connected to the stars and began communicating with light-beings. I was ready; the inquisitive search for my truth had lain dormant for too long and I leapt in without looking. Feeling as if I was coming in from the cold, my awakening, like new spring buds, was bringing in a new energy that felt like a homecoming. As I had begun to find the riches that were there in my heart all the time I could sense the alchemist's story as my own and feel it resonating in the hearts of all those accompanying me on this universal journey.

Knowing that through the Aries archetype we can discover our creative spirit; the treasure that we all carry within us, it was not surprising that this allegorical story of the man from Somerset was so appealing to me. However, it wasn't until I returned home to my house in Somerset and looked out of my window at my beautiful garden, which had a blossoming plum tree in the middle of it, that its whole truth hit me. It had taken nearly a week for me to make this connection, under my nose in my own back garden, just to push the message firmly home.

However, there were more stories to bring in. I had already been learning Reiki healing and working with chakra energy; this is an Eastern spiritual belief system that teaches about energy fields within and around our physical bodies. Chakras (the word means 'wheels') are energy centres, seven of which are located along the spinal cord from its base to the crown of the head. Each centre is a vortex of spirally energy, called *prana* or *chi* in different traditions, meaning 'life force'. These seven vortices are vibrating; some believe that their frequencies relate to the colours of the rainbow, and I have also come to understand that they can be related to the notes of a rising musical scale.

In Chloe Goodchild's project *The Naked Voice*, she explains that the voice, as vibration, is the manifestation of our silent vibration, the essence of our being. She teaches that the beginning of any journey – whether it is the beginning of a year, of a new relationship or a new life – corresponds to the root or base chakra and the first colour in the rainbow spectrum. Our journey comes from source, prior to its birth, and progresses 'through the birthing canal' into life, where it reaches the second, sacral chakra. This is where our creative energy can be found and it corresponds to our reproductive organs, and we move from the colour red to orange. From here we can continue to travel through the energy of each chakra as our experience unfolds. Chloe Goodchild correlates life's journey with a music scale, with the first note associated with the root chakra. As we sing through the notes of each chakra we are recalibrating and therefore healing ourselves. And as we heal, we can learn to be like the birds, singing our joy with the birth of the day.

As I recalled sitting by my patio doors, looking out on my

garden with the beautiful plum tree, I reflected on the shrub with its leaves coming through red in colour, and watching them, as they grow, turn to green – just like the chakras travel through the colours of the rainbow from red at the root to the green heart chakra. This beautiful representation of Mother Nature bursting into life, with all the fiery inspiration of the creative spark of spring and of Aries, awoke my curiosity. I asked a friend knowledgeable in these matters about the shrub's name. She told me its proper name was Photinia, but when the conversation developed into why I wanted to know she suddenly remembered it is also known as 'fire-bush'; perfect.

The astrologer A. T. Mann, who created the map show-ing connections between all life journeys, whether they be a single year, a human lifetime or the journey of the whole human race, shows that the first month represents just the first three months of human life. At this stage, starting at the Spring Equinox and reflecting the quick-fire energy of Aries, life is only concerned with the birth; the pure creative im-pulse, like the striking of a match. When the root chakra is open we come into life with a feeling of being very connected to our roots; Mother Earth is guiding us through this beautiful process. However, there is a shadow side to this sign and it is linked to the idea that when this chakra is closed, we become disconnected culturally and only concerned with the self. This can make the birthing process dangerous for both mother and child and the experience is one of fear. Sadly, this has shaped a large part of our cultural persona today.

With all this information flooding in, the dots were joining up for me in every direction. I'm sure we all experience that feeling at some point in our lives, when we sense that we are in the flow and all roads are coming together, offering signposts that actually sing the same song, just with a variety of melodies.

One year later, when I was working as a classroom teacher, a school project studying the planets was suggested; a planetarium was brought into the school hall and we sang songs about the planets. I was then asked to invite the children to compose their own equivalent of Holst's *The Planets*. What a gift. While I was investigating all the different scientific facts I needed for the children, I came across a lovely ancient Greek story.

Uranus, the god of the sky, married Gaia, Mother Earth. This union created the birth of Saturn, who in turn fathered Jupiter, who in turn fathered all the other inner planets. With Earth at its centre, this is how the solar system was born.

This was the Greek 'Genesis' story, their Aries journey. This has logic, as Uranus, being invisible to the naked eye and not discovered until 1781, takes the role as their invisible creative force and Saturn, being the outermost of the visible planets, would have been symbolically thrown out first, followed by Jupiter and then Mars, Venus and Mercury.

While I was putting this project together for the children, I chanced to see a science programme on television about meteors. They showed a piece of rock that had landed on the Earth soon after it came into being, about four billion years ago. It was implied that this rock, or other similar meteors, could have instigated life on Earth. This idea that life was given to us by alien means is not new, but to actually see the 'seed' in the presenter's hand was quite amazing. With the Greek story in the forefront of my mind, I came to see how the two stories were really the same. On the one hand we have the scientists' understanding that Mother Earth was seeded with life, like an egg fertilised by a sperm, by a small meteor that came flying in from outer space. On the other hand the Greeks talked about Mother Earth bringing about life as she was seeded by the sky god. It's the same story, just a different way of telling it, and it's up to us to choose which style of information we relate to.

Each of our lives is a story and these stories are so much easier to digest and relate to than mere facts, because they have a flow, a meaning and give a sense of purpose to our lives. We owe much to the Greeks and other ancient peoples who used storytelling. It is a custom still very much present in indigenous cultures today, and it is certainly re-emerging in some new alternative practices. But many are drawn to the contemporary stories around the world because they are visible. However, for the West these are not our stories. Although the stories are relevant and beautiful, it is often more beneficial to seek out the stories that belong to our own land, that feed our roots. Here in Britain we have a history steeped in stories and wisdom that has been lost. The Celts understood the many levels of their physical and spiritual journey and lived harmoniously with their spiritual truth and the land, but we have forgotten most of their folklore over the centuries. It is time to dig deep into our own roots and remember what came before us, as I fear that those who adhere solely to our present Western scientific methodology are in danger of losing their way.

Let us bring stories back into our lives and take this first step, like the burst of life in springtime, with the energy of the first chakra and Aries igniting sparks of creativity and inspiration within us.

Chapter 2

My Cup Flows Over

Give It Up

I bought some land and the land was living,
I felt its heart beat inside of me,
It fed my soul just what I needed,
Did I own it or did it own me?

Sunrise, sundown, the circles guide me,
Nature's banquet, the gift is free,
I know you want to give it value,
But land is older than currency.

Give it up, let it go,
Let the flowers grow and the rivers flow,
Give it up, let it go, it's not a marketplace,
Just a beautiful show.

We came from the land and the land was giving,
But we learnt to live independently,
We paved paradise and we built our cities,

And put a price tag on all we see.
They're selling pieces of the moon,
And wonders never cease,
Do you want a piece of the moon
Even though it's the wrong kind of peace?

Have we lost our way in this concrete jungle?
A yearning heart grows needy.
The need it grows and the price is rising,
So we file our hearts up for bankruptcy.

Give it up, let it go,
Let the flowers grow and the rivers flow,
Give it up, let it go, it's not a marketplace,
Just a beautiful show.

As we reach the second step on our journey, from the month beginning the 21st of April, the spring buds are turning to blossom and Mother Earth is brimming with life; she is abundant. For some, this is the most beautiful time of year. This exquisite, feminine energy of Mother Nature is the universe showing off its creativity in full flow, the great breathing out of all her glory.

Beltane is the Pagan festival held at this time of year which encourages us to dance around the maypole and enjoy the fertility and beauty of nature and our part in it. As we have arrived fully in our sacral chakra, situated a couple of inches below our belly button, we are experiencing the fullness and fecundity of Mother Earth and the gifts she bestows upon us. We are invited to take our fill; to be immersed in the richness of all she offers. There is a strong sexual nature in festivals at this time of year, and the May Queen is chosen for her beauty and then crowned. We can rejoice in the wonder and joy of the act of sexual intercourse and reproduction; the fruit of this gift.

This is something to be celebrated and immensely grateful for. Sadly, I have been feeling for too long that this lies at the heart of our problems as a culture. Sensing that we have forgotten how to celebrate with her, having little comprehension of the need to show our gratitude, our modern urban lifestyles are a million miles from the lives of our ancestors. Thinking we know so much more, we now view those that came before us as ignorant peasants. The irony of this is profound, and when we are ready to learn from our past and remember what we have lost we will gain much. Many are already on this journey, and it starts with simplicity and gratitude.

As we have journeyed away from spirit, away from God and our understanding of the true workings of the universe, I believe we now find ourselves in a place of separation and judgement with all things. Our relationship with sex was one of the first concepts to come under fire with the teaching of the idea of 'original sin'. The judgement has replaced our feeling regarding the sexual experience, going from one of rapture to guilt and fear in the extreme, and even for the many it saddens me that, in our society, we don't really know what a complete and truly open-hearted relationship with sex and love means. The sense of pain and loss that the absence of this experience has left has created a hole in our belly the size of an ocean, which we are constantly trying to fill. Deep in our hearts we all know that reconnecting with Mother Earth and the love she bestows is the only thing that can fill this void, and for those that can feel this, it is rising like a great sea.

So that I could attempt to ride this tidal wave with a broader understanding of what is happening here, I began contemplating the archetypal aspects of the second astrological sign of Taurus. It is an earth sign, a feminine, negative, receptive sign, which represents matter, possessions and owning or having. It is ruled by our planet Earth, which feeds us and gives us the air to breathe, filling us with abundance; our very own manna from heaven.

The map created by A. T. Mann showed me that this month represents the age of the child from three months to two years in our lifetime journey. It is in this stage of life that we are hopefully having all our needs met in this beautiful, simple time of life. This enables us to carry this feeling of being held through our whole life experience. This totally reflected all my findings with such beautiful synchronicity, enabling me to wrap myself deeply in it all. We are being invited to completely immerse ourselves in the connection with the mother – our own mother and Mother Nature. But how many of us truly know this?

Being ever the optimist, our comprehension and perspective need to be clear on our healing journey, so at this point, I feel it is important to remember that although the feminine archetypes are described as being negative, the word 'negative' is just a state of being that is, as it's used in physics, opposite to positive, like high and low, cold and hot or shadow and light. We have attributed 'good' and 'bad' connotations to these words and in doing so have learned to fear certain aspects of life, avoiding and ignoring these issues rather than having the courage to face them. We need to remember that all these extremes are part of a spectrum which all of humanity has to experience to fully understand itself and grow. The more we choose not to face our fears, the more these so-called 'negative' aspects of our culture begin to take a hold, casting a great shadow on our lives even though we believe we're not looking at them. I feel our society has fully embraced the shadow side of this archetype, giving us this feeling of lack of abundance and lack of connection. However, it is important not to apportion blame or judgement; moreover we should recognise that this is part of the process of discovering ourselves, so that we can reach a point where we choose to return home.

I sense that this has been a slow, painful journey, and I do believe the ancients understood the relationship that is ever present between humans and Mother Earth. They understood how to live alongside her cycles, appreciate her gifts and not abuse her offerings. However, Greek mythology tells how Perseus severed the head of the Medusa, beginning the journey into the illusion that we have cut the connection. Medusa is portrayed nowadays as a symbol of evil and ugliness. So ugly, in fact, that it would kill you just to cast your eyes upon her. In ancient times, however, Medusa's head of snakes symbolised fertility and wisdom and the feminine; the Goddess or the mother. Until now, we have chosen to hold on to the feeling of separation and written this part of the story out of our tales and knowledge of ancient times. I only chanced upon this extended version in my twenties.

So now having become firmly fixed in this way of being detached from Mother Earth and the love she offers, not only is there a void in our bellies where that connection was, but the void has been there so long we've forgotten what was once there. As parents, when we are in that enchanting relationship with our baby, the only thing that baby needs, other than obvious things like food and warmth, is that deep connection, especially with the mother; to know love and see it reflected in their eyes. Unfortunately too many parents get caught up in believing their children need 'things' to make them happy. When the love, and I mean that deep knowledge and openness to love, is present in a child's upbringing, the child will be filled with contentment. When love is missing, children often try to fill that gap with things and can fall into the trap of stealing. There should be no blame, for even if one tries to blame the parents for not offering the love their children needed, often it can be the case that they were not given it by their own parents. If they do not know it, how can they be expected to pass it on? This cycle needs to be broken and I feel we can start by bringing back the full understanding of our ancient May Day celebrations and reconnecting with the joys that this time of year brings into our culture. We can fall in love all over again and begin to get back in touch with the wonders of our physical sense of self and abundance that the Earth bestows.

However, there are many who are not ready to be open to these ideas, as self-love is very low on our personal agendas. We have become a society of consumers, grown out of a need to constantly fill the void created by the absence of Mother Earth. With our amnesia, now all we can sense is that it is something to do with possessions, matter and owning. So what do we do? We go shopping; or even stealing. Our need for possessions has now truly got out of hand as we seem to have put a price tag on everything, and have lost a sense of reason and proportion of what anything is worth. Although many have long recognised that money is at the heart of this, culturally, we have forgotten that money is just a tool, a flow of energy that can move freely in and out of our lives. When we truly understand this, we can become less attached to it so it can become just a means to an end, not the end in itself. However much we know, deep inside, that money, and the things it buys, will not fill the void, our loss of connection to Mother Earth's inner wisdom will not let us, as a society, hear this truth; we keep filling our houses with things we don't need. If you are already on your journey then you may well be among those who feel greatly concerned that consumerism is damaging the very being we need to be more connected to: our Earth.

As we develop an increasingly irrational attachment to money, we have started dealing in commodities that do not belong to us. We have been buying and selling land for a long time now; the indigenous peoples find this incomprehensible and now it seems we have really taken this to the extreme. I once saw a programme about a man who had found a loophole in the law, patented the moon and was selling pieces of it. People were actually willing to buy a piece of the moon. What lunacy. Ironically, the moon in astrology symbolises the inner feminine, the mother, and it also symbolises our true nature. Wanting to connect symbolically with the moon is what we actually need to be doing. But we don't need to buy it. We already own it; it is who we truly are. It is that old alchemist's journey again: we have had to lose it, and go on a journey, to be able to return home and find it was there all along. It was this story that inspired my song *Give It Up*.

What was important for me was that I, for the first time in my life, became aware that I have my moon in Taurus and so this sign symbolised the true essence of who I am. Having been sold the ridiculousness of the horoscope before this course, I had only ever been aware of my sun sign, which represents the ego, and had tried to attribute everything that I was to that sign. No wonder I was not particularly drawn to astrology before. Pisceans are watery – emotional, yes, that was me; artistic, yes, that's me too; but dreamers? I was never a dreamer. Down to earth and scarily pragmatic is how I'd have described myself. Discovering I had my moon in Taurus suddenly made it all make sense; I had that feeling of being grounded at last. However, I knew there was a lack of flow in my life and healing this part of the narrative began to hold real importance for me. I also learned that my north node is also in Taurus. Our south and north nodes represent where we have come from and where we are headed. If we get stuck in our past issues, our south node, we can often have problems moving forward in our lives. Knowing that we are all destined to step into our north node, which for me meant abundance, certainly helped me find my way forward.

First, I sensed I was going to have to face and maybe

wrestle with my negativity towards money. Many of us go through life with this problem, in an array of varying degrees. Some do not know how to control the amount they bring in, some feel they never have enough however much they earn, and some can never seem to bring much in at all. I certainly belonged to the latter, on one level, and as I began to address this, the synchronicities again began to pop up, as you may have experienced.

I have for many years now understood that when you hold on to a fear of anything, you are actually bringing what you fear closer to you. You are attracting it by the fact that you are dwelling on the matter: like attracts like. As soon as you learn to let go of the fear (in my case it was the fear of not having enough money), the energy is allowed to flow and money naturally comes more easily. However, I seemed to have a double-sided block: alongside my fear I was also holding on to a lot of guilt. This is such a multi-layered emotion tied up with being Jewish, which starts with guilt about surviving the Holocaust. This then pervades through the layers of your life, and for me, having had such a wonderful childhood, I was already feeling guilt by the age of eighteen. So even when I did start bringing money into my life and felt a flow of energy, there always followed a feeling of unworthiness and more blocks would appear. It is an amazing revelation when you realise that there is really only one story, but that we each have our own version of living it out. Like many of us, I knew it would take many experiences to overcome all these factors I was holding on to.

One simple event started the ball rolling, but it took many such events before I fully trusted it. I was receiving a healing from a wonderful crystal healer friend, Louise Chalice.

At the end of the session she said, "There is a crystal here for you, use your pendulum to find it."

I had been using a crystal pendulum for some time, using

it as a dowser searches for water beneath the surface of the ground. The pendulum works in the same way by searching for answers beneath your conscious mind. If you ask the questions in the right way you can receive amazing 'yes' or 'no' answers direct from a higher dimensional version of yourself. Although I had enjoyed working with this for a year or so, I was also slow to trust myself at times. My pendulum did, typically, choose one of the largest, most expensive crystals on the shelf, and I could feel myself tighten with discomfort. Knowing that my pendulum's choice was really just my true choice without any attachment to fear, I still questioned how I was going to find the £33 for the crystal. My friend told me not to worry; this powerful crystal had chosen me, not the other way around, and so it would wait as long as it took till I had the money.

I told her that at the weekend I had a little gig that might bring in a proportion of the money needed and asked if I could pay it off in instalments. She kindly agreed. The gig was an acoustic night with a trio I played with and the payment was based on a hat that went round. I was expecting my share to be about £10. When the gig was over I learned that I had been wrongly informed about our fee and actually the pub would be putting in £60 on top of the hat; so things were looking up. As the money was counted from the hat it added up to £40 – you can see where this is heading. The two amounts together came to £100 and divided by three, I came away with £33.

Now I know this is no great revelation and some may just say it is a happy coincidence. But to me a coincidence is not a thing of chance but a coming together of events; a convergence of energy as the universe is working with you. Even the world of science agrees that there is an interlocking web of energy that ripples through everything, whether it is understood to be the magnetic field or gravitational pull that holds everything together or our quantum world of particles, quarks and photons that exist throughout. I do not feel it is my place to understand it theoretically, although I'll give it a damn good go, but I do feel we can all learn to live within its synchronistic flow and enjoy the delights it offers us. The beauty is that once you start to engage and trust, it becomes a constant stream.

What I gained from this simple experience was that if I was in need of something that was for a greater purpose or just a purpose that would serve me, then the universe would work with me to make sure I had the money for it. Knowing that removing any sense of fear of not being able to bring the money in, or guilt that we don't deserve it, shows how we can be in harmony with the world around us and allow the right energy to flow into our lives. This can bring an amazing sense of comfort and trust in ourselves, and a feeling of optimism, knowing that we are being looked after. Of course this is an everyman's story and discovering it for myself meant that my desire to bring this to whoever wanted to hear it grew with my gratitude.

With this new, clear vision of a world of abundance available to all I felt the absence of Mother Nature in our culture ever more keenly. I could see the need to fill the void her absence has created and knew that the feeling sat very powerfully in our bellies. This metaphor showed how clearly our sacral chakra also deals with our eating habits and the abundance of food.

I know so many of us live with this issue on a day-to-day basis and that at the extremes of our society, obesity and diabetes have become a major problem. (On the other end of the spectrum, anorexia and bulimia also play a frightening role in showing our need to heal this important cultural story.) Sadly we seem to only concern ourselves with curing the physical problem, rather than looking to the core issue. I do not think it takes a huge leap of the imagination to recognise that the causes of over (or under) eating are borne out of our emotions. The lack of love that we hold in our bellies is easily, but only temporarily, filled by the quick fix of comfort food. The misery that this brings as the weight piles on only compounds the problem. Only by reconnecting to Mother Earth can she hold and embrace us in the way that fills our hearts and makes us feel that we are not alone, answering all our needs so that we no longer hunger for love. Connecting to this archetypal aspect of my nature has silently worked its magic all through my life ever since.

Although my relationship with money had brought its challenges, my relationship with food didn't seem such a huge problem, but I still had my demons. I have always felt loved and supported in my life and for this I am hugely grateful. However, although I had no addictions, as with my issue with money, guilt was playing its part and I always struggled to put the weight on. Although some find this extremely annoying it is actually something that has needed investigation to bring about the healing of my whole life story. Releasing myself from the discomfort of living well and learning to live in state of abundance with the banquet of food that Mother Nature offers was an important lesson for me, and was also going to need much prompting from my angels.

A pendulum may seem like a New Age invention but it is something that has been around for thousands of years. I was beginning to feel quite attached to mine. Even though I was constantly being told that you don't always need it and you can hear by just listening to your heart, I found it always comes in handy when your mind is working overtime or if you're like me, a Pisces, for whom there are always two fish swimming quite happily in opposite directions. Decision-making was never my strength and at the dinner table, wrestling with what I would like to eat and what I feel I should eat would be a constant dilemma. Balancing the knowledge that people were dying daily from starvation, yet it was in my highest good to step into my abundance, kept me see-sawing from decision to decision. Luckily for me my abundant self has had the loudest voice and although guilt has never eaten away at my appetite it has prevented me from storing food; 'hollow legs' has been a description I have heard all too frequently.

One day I was with my friend Seb and she wanted to treat me to lunch. Seb has always understood the flow of money and has always been very generous with it, even though she generally has little. We were on the desserts and once again I was faced with making a decision. Should it be the pavlova or the pecan pie? Now one of my downfalls is my tendency to be overly serious. If there is one message my angels are constantly trying to get through to me, it is to 'lighten up'. I reached for my pendulum. I had been using it long enough by now not to be embarrassed to get it out in public. It gave a very definite answer that we should order the pecan pie. Seb and I looked at each other and knew exactly what the other was thinking. Now a decision had been made for us, we didn't want it. We wanted the pavlova. We decided that although the guidance had been given, we were still allowed free will, whether it was for our own good or not. This is something man has always had, and whether you see it as our weakness or just our chance to take a more eventful road, that is your choice and always will be. However, this time, I sensed it was accompanied by a slice of guilt, which I quickly pushed aside.

We called the waitress and ordered our pavlova, happy in the knowledge that we had made the right decision. Five minutes later the waitress returned apologising because the pavlova was finished. Of course the pendulum knew all along. We had to have the pecan pie. I could hear my angels laughing; I like to think they were laughing *with* me as well as *at* me. A sound we can all enjoy.

Most importantly, this gentle story of simple synchronicity taught me to let go of many of the thought processes I was going through whenever I was meant to simply receive. This everyman's story was speaking to me loud and clear and my pendulum was showing me that personal joy offered the world far more healing than personal angst. I was being gently ticked off from upstairs, and being shown that the sooner we let go of the worry and guilt associated with a gift we are being offered from Mother Earth, the sooner we can get on with our journey home. I am reminded of the contented Buddha, who is always shown as rather chubby.[1]

However, it is also important to remove all the self-destructive aspects of our eating habits so that we can stop projecting these emotions on to our beautiful Earth. How we work with the land is vital for our survival with our overpopulated planet. Working the land mindfully, remembering the old wisdom of how to keep the soil filled with nutrition, is something we are already losing and our desire to farm and eat well is becoming a distant memory as our habits become more dysfunctional. We can only begin to turn this around when we choose to respect ourselves, what we put in our bellies and Mother Earth.

I truly believe that the more we listen to our hearts and accept the need to change our direction on the path we have chosen, a feeling of abundance will begin to grow inside us. With that growth comes a feeling of warmth and a greater sense of joy we can all share. The lighter our hearts, the less 'stuff' we will need to make us happy. As possessions or things hold less value in our lives, a feeling of co-operating with Mother Earth rather than stripping her of all she possesses will, I hope, become more important to all.

As I work harder at bringing myself into a world of integrity, I have found myself needing to live in a way of growing simplicity; yet it is an ongoing course of action that does not abate as it creates many contradictions. This is the harsh reality that is our self-created, Western culture today. As I began to put my *Keys to the Golden City* project together, I chose to leave the stability of my schoolteaching work, and I realised I was being challenged on every level. I decided to develop the performance into a healing workshop, but every time I put a workshop exercise together I was being asked to experience and release the lesson fully myself; how can I teach something that I haven't learned first? The first challenge was my relationship to money, and if I thought I was living on the edge before, from the summer of 2010 onwards I was dealing day to day with my relationship with debt, the physical reality and the stigma of it. My project was being very well received, but was working only on a very small scale. I knew I wouldn't be able to see it grow and see any financial reward until I'd ticked this particular box.

I spent the subsequent year releasing some of my innermost fears. I had recently split from a long-term relationship; the break-up proving to be painful and heart-rending. The feeling of disbelief that we had come so far but had still lost our way was making the process harder to bear. However, we somehow found the strength and made sure that as we started as friends, we were determined to come through it as friends. This was thankfully achieved, and with much love.

So, I found myself in the summer of 2011 living alone, stripped back to the bare essentials in love and money. I was managing to live in my beautiful house as simply as I could, with no change of income whilst trying to get to grips with the debt I had incurred. With this new sense of contentment, I felt this was reflected in my garden, which was now showing early signs of growth. It was with great excitement that I watched my fruit and vegetables in their blossoming potential. In my new solitude, in my now silent house, in one of the quietest and, I believe, most beautiful villages in the country, I finally reached a place where I felt I had everything I could possibly want: a roof over my head, clothes on my back and a real sense of fulfilment within. Less truly becomes so much more.

By the spring of 2011, I was at last feeling aligned with my Taurus moon, my true abundant self. As I reflect back I see how I have constantly battled with trying to come to terms with my sense of dismay at what we are doing to the Earth. It is a constant struggle for all to, on one side, want more money to flow into our lives, and on the other side, be aware of what we do with our wealth and what it can destroy environmentally if we do not behave responsibly with it. The more I was able to connect with the energy of Mother Earth, the more I was able to detach myself from ego and fear. Knowing that I could not influence what others do, I contented myself with the fact that I could only work on myself and reflect that energy to the outside world. It was Deepak Chopra who said that everyone is doing the best they possibly can at any given moment with the tools they have available to them.[2] When I understood that, I realised no judgements could be made, even when I heard that the price of food was going to double partially due to those playing the markets. It is so easy to step into a feeling of anger when we hear such statements. I know I've felt a good deal of anger towards our political and economic affairs as a young adult.

As we learn to find peace within as a community we will realise that individuals must make their own way and draw their own conclusions. Those who are living very much in the energy of separation are like people who have become so dehydrated their body doesn't even recognise they're thirsty. I believe those who are not acting in the interests of the world as a whole will come to understand that pain when enough people find their connection again and shine that energy back at them. Then we can hope that they will choose to heal and find their way back to the community; the community of the human race in a relationship with Mother Earth.

However, there was one issue I was having trouble shifting. For a while I was coming across people who kept telling me to value myself more and ask for more money for my workshops than I had planned; they kept reminding me that the Earth is ever abundant. I know this is energetically valid and do completely agree with them on one level, but on another, the materialistic level, I felt very uncomfortable about it; one of the many reasons being that those I most wanted to reach might not be able to afford this increased rate.

It was while I was deliberating on this that I was gifted an answer. I met a wonderful psychic woman, more of whom I will speak later, who put a book into my hands, saying, "I was guided to give you this." It offered me huge answers to many of my questions. It was Paul Coelho's *The Valkyries*. In this book, the central character is searching for his guardian angel.

He meets a woman in a café after he has met his angel and she says to him, *"Someone once said that the earth produces enough to satisfy needs, but not enough to satisfy greed."*[3]

I believe that someone was Mahatma Ghandi. I need say no more.

Chapter 3

Making Air Waves

The Silent Millions

I heard a man worked for years to bring us Peace One Day.
But his story took four years to come my way.
I thought news travelled fast,
So why does the good come last?

Now we all think this world is turning inside out.
Too much pain and hurt, some need to scream and shout.
We hear too much too soon,
So we think it's all darkness and gloom.
So I throw the papers away, nothing decent in them anyway.

No news is good news,
Doesn't mean nothing good happens anymore.
The Silent Millions
Are quietly doing their thing by the open door.

Now it's all just a case of perception,
And though it don't seem quite like perfection,

Remember what makes news,
And that it's just the work of the noisy few.
So I throw the papers away, hurts my ears anyway.

———

No news is good news,
Doesn't mean nothing good happens anymore.
The Silent Millions
Are quietly doing their thing by the open door.

Is it our inclination to be hooked on sensation?
I don't read the news anymore, I just live by that open door.

No news is good news,
Doesn't mean nothing good happens anymore.
The Silent Millions
Are quietly doing their thing by the open door.

Arriving at the third stage, from May the 21st as it slips into June, there is much excitement because at last the flowers are out, with all the sensory pleasures that this offers. Following the individual process that each plant and bud has gone through to come into being, now the growth is expanding into the realms of an awareness of the other. With this comes the arrival of the bees going from flower to flower, pollinating, connecting, communicating. The art of communication is a very complex affair and if we would take the time to notice the intricacies that Mother Nature demonstrates, you can see just how mind-blowing and fine-tuned the balance is all the way up and down the food chain. I believe Mother Nature is continually showing us and teaching us how it can be done, how each animal, insect or element interacts with others to ensure its life cycle continues.

The irony is not lost on me in the way that we often run away from bees, scared of what one bee might do to us whilst not thinking of how, simultaneously, we are creating a disaster for the whole bee population, potentially upsetting the whole balance of life. If we took time to study and enjoy the way the bee gathers its nectar and then hovers in the slipstream of a gentle current of air, or how a seed is caught on an eddy of a breeze, being carried to its new point of destination, then perhaps we could learn to honour the whole process and wonder at the beautiful dance that ensues rather than being intent, as a culture, on destroying it.

Being very aware that stepping into the archetypal aspects of what this time of year had to offer was again going to be a rich journey of healing and openings, I wanted to take a look at the astrological aspects of this month. Gemini is an air sign, a masculine, positive sign. It is ruled by Mercury, the messenger and the trickster, being affiliated with thought and conscious communication. Being the first of the air signs, the communication, I feel, is between the twins, the id and the ego, the self and the inner or higher self. The curiosity of our highly stimulated and somewhat fickle minds, like the butterfly or the busy bee flitting from flower to flower, affiliates this energy, this passion for seeking knowledge, with the media; the symbol of Gemini.

A. T. Mann shows us that we have now reached the age of three on our lifetime journey. We will be here until we reach seven; infant school age, and we have separated from our mothers a little and are beginning to be fully conscious, communicating beings. It's a very exciting time and we are now gaining our first sense of independence. We are no longer a babe in arms, where we were almost completely absorbed in our relationship with our mother. We are now widening our horizons, from being toddlers to a little being, fully engaged in thought and speech. We have everything to say, many questions to ask and many new relationships to build.

Our culture, over the centuries, has already put a good deal of energy into analysing and understanding communication, but it is important to consider the breadth of the landscape when dipping your toes in, as it covers such a broad spectrum, from the personal to the interpersonal, all the way to the international.

I could see that our need to communicate is one of our oldest attributes and although we have learned to copy the beauty of nature we have also learned to twist its divinity, creating a world of deceit and distorted truths that is our media today. However, we need to take some responsibility here.

As I have become aware of our long history and how we have moved away from our spiritual journey, possibly even since the great flood, it was the end of the Age of Gemini, four thousand years ago, when we began to embrace communication more fully. The Greeks had their stories and the Jews began writing their scriptures, but both moved into a view of the world that created gods that were judgemental. Gods before this time were very much a part of us, not apart from us, but a rift had been created and we began our slow journey into the illusion of being separate from God.

What was written was held up as truth and even Jesus, who came to remind us of the way of the ancients, couldn't steer us back home. There were some around him that understood his truth but most of his disciples only got it in part, and so the new gospel only contained the new teachings that suited the times. The gospels of those that understood him fully were hidden for another two thousand years. I sense that Jesus knew he was ahead of his time and was simply sowing a seed for an age to come. The new Bible was declared to be his word and even those words got twisted through the centuries and translated to the tune of the king of the day, losing a little more of the truth each time. The recent discovery of the gospel of Thomas, I believe, reveals this perfectly and it allows us to recognise just how far we have travelled. He truly understood the word of God that Jesus spoke of.

Just as we have an amazing ability to communicate in ways that are subtle, powerful and joyful, weaving words and creating works of astounding profundity and wit, we are also capable of shutting down our talents here. I do fear that the beauty and art of communication is something we are, culturally, turning our back on.

If our way to God is through communication of the emotions and Mercury, as the archetype here, is tricking us into believing that the way to happiness is through our computers or mobile phones, then we are surely taking the hardest journey home. As we lock into the illusionary world of connecting through the airwaves rather than face-to-face, and as our words get reduced to bite-sized chunks in the form of texts, then we become lonelier and lonelier and the chance of misinterpretation and being misled grows. But don't shoot the messenger. Mercury, like all the archetypes, has two sides: the shadow and the light. The variety of channels available to us is plentiful. We can choose to connect at the personal level as much as is possible, and like the bee, get out in our community and be with people, or we can choose not to. I do not have a problem with technology. It offers so much potential for good and a lifeline for so many; I am simply aware of the potential for misuse, as with all things, that we know is happening all around us.

I do not want to get too caught up in the shadow aspect of our media, as I believe we create what we have in our lives by the power of our thoughts. So it was concentrating on its positive attributes that led me to the story behind my song, which in turn enabled me to start addressing my desire to expand my own field of communication.

It was 2005 when I heard about the wonderful young man Jeremy Gilley, who worked very hard for several years to bring Peace One Day into existence, a day of global peace recognised by the UN in 2001. I naively presumed this would be a cause for celebration, but it took four years before it came to my notice and I am still amazed that so many people are still unaware of it even today. I realised that the media isn't interested in news with a happy ending, because that simply doesn't sell as well as tragedy. I began to see with new eyes how it feeds off our fear and need for sensationalism. As it's never going to change by itself, it will be up to us to make the shift in our own lives first. I had already started as I stopped buying the papers a long time ago. I knew then I would have to keep my ear closer to the ground if I wanted to hear any good news, and I know now that change will only come from the people at grass-roots level, not from the institutions. As we, as a nation, become increasingly aware that what we read in the papers or hear on the television is not the real truth at all, I believe we will eventually realise that there is no point taking on board information that doesn't serve us. As we are the ones fuelling the industry as we continue to buy the newspapers, we also have the power to pull the plug. This will not come a moment too soon.

However, there are of course many people, like Jeremy Gilley, who are working to transform the content of our news by creating good news worth telling, and there are also others who are intent on bringing the good news to us, as there is always plenty to spread. There is now a paper called *Positive News* in publication, and many online positive news websites, all of which fill me with hope. I wrote the song *The Silent Millions* to highlight the need to concentrate on the positive aspects of our world alongside the awareness that we are constantly being drawn to the tragedy as this reflects our own feelings of fear. The sooner we decide we can choose a better way – by choosing to find peace within to create that peace without – the sooner our media will start to reflect this and communicate this change rapidly through our global network. How we go about this is proving to be a rocky road but I am ever hopeful that our new form of social activism can provide the roots to this story.

Knowing that change can only come from us as individuals, looking at it from this perspective, I could sense the complexity. We all bring our own story to the table like the amazing variety of flowers that grow from the same soil, but how we bring these stories together in a way that works for all, could prove interesting. Personally, mine is full of contradictions. Like everyone who comes to a juncture in their life, there is always much work to be done. I could see that I was going to have to review my internal communications before I could understand how to deal with the external problems I was having: taking my work as a musician, and emerging storyteller, out into the world.

What particularly interested me as I probed more deeply into my astrology is how beautifully my journey reflected the Gemini aspects of my chart. I could immediately see how, after my awakening, my creative energies were emerging like butterflies but I was flitting from one idea to the next. I was planting seeds all over the place but not waiting for the bud to flower before I was impatiently rushing off to the next experiment. I needed to pause for thought. Looking at my chart from another angle, I could see that my Jupiter is in Gemini and Jupiter takes the role of the father. The expansive nature of Jupiter, the king of the Grecian gods, in Gemini showed me that my potential as a communicator was yet to be unveiled, and I was soon to discover that my father was going to be helping me in all this. As with all experiences we never know this till we are in a place to stop and review.

I began to reflect on my relationship and communication with my father as he has a Gemini sun. I had a wonderful upbringing and get on wonderfully with both my parents. However, I had become aware that being placed in a household with four talkative women (I am one of three daughters), my father had always taken a bit of a back seat as far as conversations were concerned. He would often say with a wry smile that he couldn't get a word in. However, he also has a great capacity to talk with a conversational ease and is a great speech-maker. Over time, I've also begun to see him as the listener. Something I certainly aspire to be.

I had become aware that, when visiting my parents as an adult, most of the conversations took place between my mother and myself; however, a quiet connection was beginning to make itself evident as the years began to unfold. Interestingly for me, it was to be through the world of healing that the communication was going to develop. My father told me many years ago that he had been told, when he was a young man, that he had a healing gift and that he should join a group of faith healers. However, after his first visit, my father found it difficult to relate to these people, whom he said had a kind of distant look in their eyes as if they weren't really there. He never went back.

Thirty years later, when I was a teenager I remember him returning home from work one day with a story. A woman had approached him because she recognised a healing gift, that she also had, in him. My father was a little taken aback with this second occurrence so many years after the first. I was fascinated but like him, I didn't believe I had any special gifts, though I remember wishing that I did. I just stored it away, as I always do with anything like this.

Twenty years later again I have my awakening. As with anything like this, if it happens to you, you feel like you are bursting with your new way of seeing the world. You want everyone you care about to see it too. It's only natural; it's a beautiful thing. You become like the true evangelist and it takes a while for you to realise, so absorbed are you in your heightened state of being, that people are removing themselves from the conversation and looking at you with concern or derision. You begin to realise that your friends and family aren't going to suddenly start thinking like you do just because you've had an amazing epiphany. In fact you realise the more you try to push it, the more they are just going to distance themselves from you. It took me six months to bring my excitement down to a manageable level. Learning how to communicate and only speak about my new ideas to those who seemed interested was going to be a big lesson to learn, and communicating with those I cared most about had to be handled with extra care.

I learned that you have to just be true to who you are and let people come to you when they were ready. I knew I could do nothing but hope.

It took two years for my father to summon up the courage and one day he came and sat next to me as I was sitting on his sofa and said, "So tell me about what you do."

I was so excited, as you can imagine. I knew I would have to breathe and choose my words carefully as this could be the make or break of a new journey my father and I could share. If I didn't take enough care in putting my ideas across, I could put him off, like those people did at the faith healing he attended all those years ago. We spoke for quite a while and he was very interested, but my father seemed to feel that at the age of seventy-seven he was too old to be taught new tricks. Happy to leave it at that for the moment, I did recall a lovely conversation when he'd asked me what I thought our mission was in life. I said I thought we should live on this Earth leaving as little mark in the world as possible, like footprints in the sand.

"Not even good deeds?" he asked. "Should we not even try to help others?"

"Well, yes, of course," I said, "but we need to be mindful of the fact that even healing isn't always appropriate."

I went on to explain that I felt that sometimes, healing prevents a person going through the lesson they need to learn in life, however dark and painful that journey may seem. In the end, I believe it's best to work on healing yourself, which will in turn inspire others to seek out their own wisdom and healing for themselves. That's the greatest gift you can bring to the world.

It did make me stop and question my desire to become a healer. Was I right to do so? It's a question I have to keep asking myself. Is healing always appropriate? I understood that healing had to be asked for; only the recipient knows when they are ready to take that journey. That seemed to satisfy my unsettled feelings as well as reminding myself that a healer is only offering a space for the recipient to find their own body wisdom. Rather like the doctor that applies a cast to a broken bone thinking he has fixed it; he has done nothing except shore up the bone, so the body can continue its own healing. It's the wisdom of our metabolism that is doing all the work, knitting the bones together and regrowing the skin and tissue.

A couple of years slipped by and although it always came up in conversation I felt I couldn't give my words enough weight to change his perception or his need to expand his life story. Nothing, as far as I was concerned, was shifting for my father. I was beginning to wonder if the only way to draw him into his healing journey, if indeed, he needed to be drawn, would be out of necessity. Suddenly there it was, and my mother was saying, very quietly and understatedly, that she had to go into hospital to have a lump removed from her leg. We're not worriers, generally, and it was all taken in a very low-key manner, thank goodness, as it needed no more treatment than this small operation.

Knowing my father was going to be alone for a few days, I suggested that I came for lunch before going to visit Mum in hospital and if he fancied I'd give him a healing. If he enjoyed it, I suggested he might want to try offering some healing to Mum when she came out. He agreed and during the Reiki session he was able to find a very deep, relaxed physical state, which he thoroughly enjoyed. Being a very relaxed person anyway this was no revelation; the issue was that my dad didn't really see the need for offering healings.

I had spent many years learning how we communicate on a higher level, how our cells connect to the universal web of oneness, but I knew those were words that would not mean anything to my dad. I needed something that would strike a chord for him, so as we left for the hospital I tried to explain about the joy of giving and receiving on a universal level. I wasn't convinced I was getting through. As I was getting a parking ticket, with money that Dad gave me, someone approached me and offered me their ticket that they no longer needed. I went back to Dad and told him of this kind deed.

"Oh," he said, "perhaps that was because I gave my ticket to someone else yesterday."

I gave a quick hallelujah and thank you to 'upstairs', as I call my angels, and said very simply to Dad that he'd got exactly what I was trying to explain earlier. He did hear me and I knew that the universe had communicated to him in a clear and simple way where my words could not. After we'd visited Mum, he thanked me for the healing and said that I'd made the world seem like a much lovelier place. However wonderful this made me feel, patience was needed if I believed anything else might happen for my dad.

A few years later and my father and I stepped into a very interesting stage. As I began my astrology course I had just turned forty-two and my father was eighty-four – so I was half his age. He had arrived at his Uranus return (as Uranus takes eighty-four years to go round the sun) whilst I was experiencing my Uranus opposition. It is at this time that we have journeyed halfway round the cycle, finding that we are now facing the point at which we started. This creates great tension as somehow, subconsciously, we are caught in the middle but being pulled in both opposite directions at once. This is why this stage in our lives is often called the midlife crisis. I was now arriving at a halfway point on the same journey that my father was completing. Both these moments in a lifetime journey can create powerful experiences, and when a father and daughter coincide like this it can lead to a lot of fun.

Having had no success with opening my father's mind to the idea that the universe was asking him to awaken to his calling, I would have normally left it at that. However, other healers in my life started talking about his calling too, though I didn't tell him as much. Around this time I was staying at a friend's house while doing some work in their garden. One evening we were chatting and my father seemed to be coming up a lot. My friend intuitively suggested I should ask him to give me a healing rather than the other way around. I knew as soon as she said this that it was as good as done, as my father would do anything to help one of his daughters.

The next time I was at my parents' I gently brought the subject up and he agreed to 'have a go'. The next visit, I explained what I did in my healing sessions and then shared a breathing exercise which energises you in a positive way, thinking it might get him into the right frame of mind. He gave me a gentle healing, simply laying his hands on my shoulders, but neither of us had any idea if anything had occurred other than a lovely sense of bonding between us. Here was my father, my only family member happy to join me on my journey, even if it was for a short distance. I was very grateful on many levels.

The next day I went back to my friend's house to cut the lawn. It was a foot high, a very large expanse and their lawn-mower was partially broken. I worked like a dog to get it done and it nearly killed me. Eventually I had to stop as I was due at work and needed a shower. Well, I looked in the mirror and was astounded. I saw something I hadn't seen for sixteen years. My face was completely mulberry-coloured. I have been experiencing asthma since I was twenty-six and this only used to happen before I became asthmatic, when I really physically pushed myself. With asthma, my breathing difficulties would always kick in way before I'd get to this stage, preventing me from ever really exerting myself. Was I cured?

I waited a few days before saying anything to Dad, but sadly the asthma did return. I was then reluctant to say anything until Mum asked about a week later, "Your father's too shy to ask, but did anything come of that healing?"

I explained what had happened and I expressed my gratitude even though the result was short-lived. A week or so later we arranged another session. This time, as we started the same breathing exercise as before, my father completely slipped off somewhere. He seemed to reach a deep mental state which was a whole new experience and totally amazed him. It seemed to me that he had opened up a channel between his conscious self and the higher energies in his auric field. This communication between the many versions of ourselves is vital for us as individuals if we wish to grow spiritually. For my father it came as a complete surprise, but one that he accepted with grace. For me, I was simply grateful that I had been able to open him into my new world without scaring him off. Was I at last learning to communicate in a way that went beyond my ego and step aside so the higher energies could do their work, teaching with more sensitivity and insight than I could ever hope to offer? He then gave me a beautiful, completely intuitive healing.

That was the last healing my father and I shared and so I decided to relate this story to Chrissy Philp, astrologer and author of *The Golden City* (the book that inspired so much of my journey). She brought up my father's chart next to mine, showing me that while my Chiron, the healer, is in a very complex position in my chart, my father's is very straightforward and clear. I understood that my need to offer healing is very deep-seated in my nature and that my methods tended to be very prescriptive. My father's Chiron, however, is in Aries; he does it without thinking, in the moment. Of course, I realise as I sit and write this now that this is why, as he keeps notching those years up, he is fit as a fiddle and always has been. There is a conjunction between his Chiron with Pluto, which means it's well hidden as Pluto is god of the underworld, and also Mercury, the messenger, ruler of Gemini, who keeps it constantly connected. It was such a beautiful moment for me to know that I really didn't have to encourage him to do anything for himself as he has always been doing it anyway. I knew I no longer had to discuss this with him on a conscious level because the discussion was constantly kept open, deep in the inner workings of his physical and etheric body, by Mercury, the king of communication.

I recalled the conversation we'd had about only needing to heal yourself to fulfil your purpose in life and how he was a perfect example, shining his health, happiness and vitality for all to see without making demands on anyone. I felt humbled, sensing I had a good deal to learn about simply being a healer as a journey of the self. The expression 'physician, heal thyself' was echoing in my ears.

As the wheel kept on turning and I arrived at this point of the yearly cycle again in the summer of 2011, John Wadsworth gave me a new insight into some of the qualities of this archetype as he very generously invited me back for more visits to his beautiful astrological Alchemical Journey. I had always thought of the archetype of Mercury as solely that of the conscious communicator. But now John explained how a Gemini could be a true channeller. We can see this as the twin playing its part; as soon as the ego gets out of the way, the chatter of the brain stills as the aspect of Mercury that is always trying to keep us distracted is momentarily hushed, and the true messenger can go straight to the heart and communicate at the deepest of levels. I believe this is where my father began to journey to when he reached that deep state with such ease, and what I constantly struggle to find. Therein lies the problem in our busy lives today, and it's 'the struggle' that is often the main obstacle. Although I simply need to release the idea of 'trying' and just do it, it is so much easier said than done.

Having put the request out, the universe soon offered me a dynamic meditation that pushes the conscious brain out of the way to allow the higher consciousness to speak. It is a twenty-one-day process that I just managed to finish the day before I left for Glastonbury Festival to work with my harp in the Peace Dome – a twenty-four-hour meditation space. The festival was amazing, but hard work on all levels. The rain and mud made it physically wearing and the hard graft meant I found it difficult to get deep into the meditation space, but the Peace Dome was working its magic and on the last day it all came together.

I was realising my problems with meditating were due to the fact that I wasn't properly aligned. My posture was bad at the base of my spine and though many people had been pointing me towards yoga, I was being too slow in getting there. With the help of two massages that made me aware of the tension I was holding around my root chakra, it was time to take responsibility to remove it. With a few simple exercises and the intense power of the Peace Dome, I released the pain and achieved a perfect meditation posture. I was ready to embark on a new journey of inner communication with myself, and to be more discerning when it came to listening to my Mercurial archetypes. I knew the trickster was always there, hoping to trip me up and draw me into the messages of fear. I wanted to concentrate my energies on only listening to messages of love.

As I returned from the festival, from the cocooned existence that I created without papers, televisions or the Internet – and my ability to shut out any conversations of the outside world – I discovered a mini revolution was taking place. It was the summer of 2011 and we had just experienced two solar eclipses, both huddled around a very powerful Summer Solstice as we left Gemini. The media had gone through quite a shift with the News of the World phone hacking scandal and people power was learning how to flex its muscles. Here was the media being questioned for its behaviour, at its most senior level, and although little came of it, I found this incredibly exciting as I have been saying all along how change will only come from the bottom up.

The steps have only been small but the tortoise has always made better progress than the hare, and I sensed that I was reflecting this as I had begun to make a small start on healing my own difficulty with taking my work into the community. I started hosting some of my three-hour introductory sound healing workshops and received an increasingly positive response. Small steps that would lead to greater leaps.

Now I could see the power of the Internet coming into play beautifully. If the media reflects the mechanics of communication, then the Internet is the communication itself. Like our brains, the computer does all the mechanical downloading of the information but the Internet, the interlocking web, reflects our connection to the ether where all information is stored. This world has always been available to us; we've just closed down those connections. Once we open up to the archetype of Mercury in us all we can see how we have created the computer and the Internet as a manifestation of what already is; a clear sign that we're already on our way. We can then switch it off and use the telepathic abilities that we've had all along. In the meantime, while we are still working mainly on the physical dimension, there are Internet sites and online groups of social activists that are alerting us to what is going on in the world, for better or worse, helping us to vote to make a change. The discovery that we have the power to do this is so liberating. I can only hope more people wake up to and begin their dialogue with their inner voice and discover its true power.

Chapter 4

The Past Revisited

Woman in Me

I'm searching for the woman in me.
I'm looking through thistles and thorns for the sleeping beauty.
Open your eyes for she's waking now,
To kiss the heart of every living soul.
And she'll find her way somehow.

It's time to leave yesterday behind.
Let her in and let the fairy tale begin.
It's time to leave yesterday behind, yesterday behind.

The river's turned to wine, so drink deep.
The bitterness of knowing now runs sweet.
Find her hidden well and your cup will run over,
She's the part of you that's real.
Return the prodigal lover.

It's time to leave yesterday behind.
Let her in and let the fairy tale begin.

It's time to leave yesterday behind, yesterday behind.

We're all searching for that perfect lover,
Who'll open our hearts and step in.
But you'll only find perfect lovers
In that place beneath your skin.

It's time to leave yesterday behind.
Let her in and let the fairy tale begin.
It's time to leave yesterday behind, yesterday behind.

It's the Summer Solstice. The sun is at its highest point in the sky, lightening up our days and giving us the warmth in our hearts that we've been craving for most of the year. We have come to the end of another cycle. For the last six months, since the Winter Solstice, we have been celebrating and anticipating the coming of the light as if it is our sole, or even soul, purpose, and now we have finally arrived; a homecoming. We can immerse ourselves in the joy of being part of the process of the great breathing out of Mother Nature; as we form and develop into the physical aspects of ourselves alongside the radiance of all the flora and fauna growing around us.

As we glory in the beauty of the divine feminine in us all, we can sink deep inside ourselves and feel the power and security she offers. She provides protection over our crops and we can feel more secure because of this. But as we watch them grow, knowing they are vulnerable to the elements and wildlife that can destroy them, this can cause us to be very inward-looking. So that we can sustain our family with food on the table we look to Mother Earth to keep watch over us just as we keep watch over our family, especially our young.

As we turn the astrological wheel, starting with Aries, the equinox on the ecliptic line, the horizontal axis, we have now arrived at the southernmost point on our journey at the vertical axis, the nadir, getting in touch with the innermost essence of who we are. Cancer is ruled by our moon, the mother, and the crab is the symbol of Cancer. Its hard shell, protects its soft belly like a mother nurtures her young, and yet again we are enticed into our place of sanctuary. This is the first water sign, again a feminine, receptive, negative sign, and a sign of the emotions.

A. T. Mann aligns this month with the child reaching junior school age, ever more independent, though still very much under the ever-watchful eye of our parents. Now, we are becoming emotionally aware beings, understanding the idea of empathy maybe for the first time, and we're gaining a wider perspective on life, family life in particular to begin with. We are learning more about our grandparents, our race, our culture and our roots, who we are and where we've come from.

It is here we can truly get in touch with our inner feminine wisdom. I believe the ancients had a strong connection to this knowledge but as I explained in Taurus, the Greeks and what our culture today has extracted from them played a part in cutting us off from this connection. In the story of Perseus, where he cuts off the head of the Medusa, we are told we will be turned to stone if we cast our eyes on her ugly head of snakes. This is not the first time the snake has been given a bad press, and I began to see how this was a very powerful way of preventing us from looking at our feminine wisdom. By continuing to look away and believing the twisted version of history we are handed down, we keep ourselves in this place of disempowerment.

As we move forward through history we see that Jesus reminded us that we are all sons and daughters of God, but I feel that the fear of the power we could regain allowed us to let priests and other religious leaders stand in between us and our knowledge of God. One thousand years later and we have the arrival of the Arabic people to the West, bringing their amazing knowledge of science. Having lived for so long, gradually losing our personal wisdom, without questioning, as our priests taught us not to, suddenly our inquisitive nature is brought to life. After another five hundred years, we arrive fully in our age of science and we begin to swing our metaphoric pendulum very firmly towards the masculine energy of our brain, pulling us all out of kilter. I am not speaking of gender here. I am referring to the aspects of our brain, carrying masculine and feminine attributes.

As the churches gradually began to lose their hold and we have journeyed through the last century with so many people holding their view of the world as atheists or agnostics, the feminine wisdom that we have within us is now just a distant memory. The general view is that we must only believe what we can see and touch; what is tangible. If we choose to believe what we can *feel*, rather than that which can only be proven by scientific methods, then we are generally laughed at.

Yet we are now approaching a new age, the Age of Aquarius, and there are rumblings amongst the people. There is a cry emerging to return the pendulum back to the centre ground and get back in touch with our feminine wisdom. However, humanity being what it is, the pendulum often has to swing far in the opposite direction before it can find the middle ground. We've tried feminism and the 'new man' and lost our understanding of true femininity and masculinity on the way. In trying to rediscover our power we have lost how and where to find it, and while women are trying to be more like men and men more like women, we are continuing to miss the mark. There is much self-awareness to regain and much healing needed. Turning this into a battle of the sexes will just create more wounds in need of repair.

As we continue to fear looking within and turn away from

the wisdom that we keep locked away, the shadow aspects of this archetype produce feelings of overprotection towards our own. We become insular and fearful of outsiders. We build gates round our homes and towers at our borders. War becomes our only means of dealing with the other, and we dare not look at what brought us to this place for fear of what the past will reflect back at us. I believe we need to trust in our strength and use this powerful energy that we all have within us to bring us out of these fearful times. First we have to be prepared to look at what is lurking in the depths of our psyche and do the inner work.

The answers lie in finding our inner balance with both our masculinity and femininity, and the huge success of *The Da Vinci Code* by Dan Brown showed how great this desire is. Many programmes and investigations tried to deny the truth and substance of the book, and all the other books written with this same theme, however this just keeps the wheels of public interest turning. It seems that what these programmes are failing to discuss is the fact that the Holy Grail is not a tangible object; it is not a cup or a descendant of Christ. These protagonists are still caught up in the world of the scientific nature of everything and try to latch on to things that are only in the physical. The true Holy Grail, and Dan Brown does state this, is the 'rose line' within us all; the feminine energy that we can all rediscover, but only in an energetic sense. Many people understand this, even if only subliminally, and this is why they do not care about the lack of physical proof, they just feel it inside. When we do awaken to this feminine energy and align it with our masculine energy, which we still have yet to discover, I believe we will take a huge step towards finding balance within and so gain an important key to our golden city.

In order that we reconnect to this feminine energy, we also need to embody the symbol of our own individual tree of life as part of our metaphysical selves, and it is a very powerful energy to dip into. It is felt that we not only contain within ourselves the many stages of childhood that we have experienced, returning to that image of the Russian dolls held within all living beings, but we also contain the cellular memory of our parents and forefathers.

Not only do we hold within our DNA the physical, genetic make-up, but also the belief structures that we live by, handed down to us through our lineage. On top of this, it is believed we inherit the emotional and karmic memory of our previous lives in our aura. All in all, it's quite a burden we take on and just making it through childhood is quite a feat. For those who do not feel comfortable with this as a construct they can believe in, there are, of course, many ways of reaching the same goal. I somehow felt like all the roads were leading me down this path, whether I wanted them to or not.

It began a few years back, around the millennium, when I realised my biological clock was beginning to tick ever louder in my ears and I was faced with a very difficult decision. Did I want to have children? I always thought that I would, but then I'd say, "I'll do it in ten years' time." As I approached thirty, the ten became five years and as I approached thirty-five, the dilemma was really upon me. My life as a musician and free spirit didn't really fit with motherhood, although countless others have managed it. I sensed the deep joy in the connection one gets from one's own child but I knew, all too clearly, how it would alter my life. It always baffled me how my friends would say, after having kids, that they hadn't realised how much it would affect their lives. Why didn't they realise? I couldn't understand it. Then it started becoming clear to me as I began to get the feeling that maybe I had been a baby machine in a past life, like one of my Russian great-grandmothers, for example. The more I thought about it, the more it made sense: I'd done it all before and remembered too much. Whereas some take to it like a duck to water, for others, parenthood is often best approached blind, with no prior knowledge. Otherwise we wouldn't have enough reproduction in the world as many would run a mile if they knew the full story before they entered into the bargain. I was, in effect, running that mile.

After a session with my crystal healing group, I asked one of the healers there, John, what he thought about my inkling about all this. He was a man who could see your past lives very clearly and I felt comfortable asking him.

"Yes," he said, "you have had that journey but I also see pain in childbirth; you have suffered too."

I didn't have to think about this for long without realising I wanted to investigate this, so I booked a session with him. Having never had a past life regression, I really didn't know what to expect. His room was very bare as he was always on the move at that time, so there was nothing to create an atmosphere. He is 'the wanderer' that inspired my song for Virgo. Having studied Drama A Level, it had made me very cynical of the theatrics created in churches and even with the mystics I had encountered as a musician in Hong Kong.

There was none of that here. Even so, with my tendency to doubt, I questioned, as I always did, whether I would get into the spirit of it all. Here was my other Pisces fish coming into play, swimming in opposition to the one that is constantly reaching for the stars. Yet with very few words and actions I began to sense something. My ability to visualise was not strong in those days and I always worried if what I was seeing was in fact my truth. What I did see in my mind was a beautiful four-poster bed in a very old house, perhaps a few hundred years ago. It was a very large house, like a manor house in beautiful grounds. The grandeur of the bed befitted a lord or lady's bedroom. John asked if I saw anything else but I saw nothing, just the bed. So he then asked me if I could feel anything; I asked the question for myself and that was it. Suddenly, I felt a big black hole in my heart space; it was so powerful the tears began to roll down my face.

John had explained at the start that I was like a spectator of the situation; although it was me in a past life I wasn't actually living it now. I could remain separate, like an actor. So, although the tears were rolling down my face and I could feel the pain, I knew it wasn't actually my pain so I was laughing at the same time at the bizarre quality of the whole situation. I then sensed that I had been in an abusive relationship and had chosen to get out of it, not to deal with it. In other words I had opted to die in childbirth, in this bed that I was being shown, to escape the pain I was experiencing in this past life.

My awareness was brought back to the room, although I also never felt I left. It was an odd sensation of being in two places at once. My feelings were that I was carrying a lot of unfinished business, having not faced my fear. John explained to me that through repressing my pain and anger in a past life, I had developed asthma in this life. Asthma is caused by unexpressed grief and this couldn't have been made clearer to me now. We then investigated my childhood and I became very aware of how I had shut down any tendencies to show anger in my life. In fact I could only remember two occurrences throughout my whole childhood, which were short-lived as I'd kept a tight lid on them.

This remained with me through adulthood and I had simply thought myself to be just 'not an angry person'. I was unaware of how much I was controlling my emotions and keeping them all stored up, and how I was now suffering from asthma because of this. Knowledge of this, sadly, was not enough to remove my asthma; a good deal more work was still needed. In fact, the opposite occurred. Eight months previously I had just begun a daily practice of breath work and this had seemed to heal my asthma. After this regression my asthma returned. John was devastated. I, however, just saw it as part of the process. I knew this understanding of my journey was definitely helping to loosen the mortar in the wall that needed to be broken down.

I felt that this was very much a universal story. Although I had chosen to arrive at this place through working with regressions I could see that many of us can investigate our ancestral line and reach the same outcome. I knew I also had this story to discover in my family line, and I could see that as a race we only have to go back a few generations to see the same shutting down of emotions. Having come through two world wars, we can clearly sense the waves of grief experienced but not expressed. It is a legacy that the whole world has passed down to their children. Even though it was through a desire to protect them from the pain the parents themselves have suffered, it has still slipped through the net genetically. Of course this emotional strangulation also plays itself out in our personalities even if we believe we are covering it up. In fact the opposite is true, for as we choose not to deal with the emotions they become like monsters in our subconscious. This is the legacy we have been handed down and I do not feel the immensity of this story is being truly recognised.

A year or so passed and one day, in the summer, my partner, Andy, expressed a desire to revisit an old house in the Cotswolds he'd been taken to as a child, on a school trip, called Snowshill Manor. It was a beautiful old manor house bought by a collector at the turn of the last century who had filled it with the most amazing furniture and objets d'art. It was now owned by the National Trust, and so we arranged a day to go.

The morning of the visit, as I prepared my breakfast, I felt a little odd but I didn't think any more of it. As we drove into the Cotswolds, it was a beautiful summer's day and the countryside was exquisite. Andy started commenting on my driving, saying I seemed distracted. We arrived safely at our destination and parked. As I got out of the car my hand was visibly shaking. This was not something I'd come across before, but I was getting an idea of what this might be all about.

Andy paid the admission and then we had to walk for about ten minutes through the grounds to the house. The setting was beautiful, but all of a sudden, I hit what I can only describe as a wall of energy. It was very powerful and without any warning, it made me burst into tears. Now, I am prone to emotional outbursts; films can easily make me cry and even adverts can bring a lump to my throat. These outbursts are usually very contained and I can keep it all to myself. This, however, was just embarrassing, in such a public place with people all around. I collected myself quickly and Andy put it down to the many battles that might have been fought in these parts. He was one to hold to the scientific view of energy and molecular memory as I do, but he didn't believe the idea that we might have past lives. However, as my inkling was growing stronger, I was beginning to dismiss any thoughts of having connected to the energy of some battle scene, other than a personal one.

As we approached the house, I mentioned the idea that I thought that this might be the house I had had my past life experience in, even though I knew he didn't believe in such a thing, but then I also began to wonder if it was old enough. I thought it had taken place in medieval times. As we entered we began marvelling at all the fabulous acquisitions this collector had made throughout his life. It was filled with such diverse items, from huge pieces of furniture to delicate china from the Far East, from penny-farthing bicycles to tiny hair combs from Africa. We discovered that the house started life as a monastery and was built in the 8th century; so it was plenty old enough. Then Andy commented that Catherine Parr's name kept coming up. I hadn't heard this but I noted it anyway.

We made our way upstairs and entered a room filled with

the largest collection of samurai artefacts outside of Japan. It was then I was overcome by a sense that something was going to happen when I entered the next room. Doubting myself, as ever, I told myself to settle down as I was obviously being a complete drama queen. However, as I stepped through the door any doubt just fell away. First, I saw a large four-poster bed, though it was not the same as the one in my regression. At the foot of the bed was a beautiful harp. This in itself would have been something if I had not, simultaneously, been hit by a second occurrence. I was met by a huge wall of energy, even more powerful than the one in the gardens. Here there was no place to hide; people were squashed into narrow corridors and I was trying desperately to duck away from anyone noticing or being embarrassed by my outburst. Slightly bewildered, Andy did his best to make sure I was all right, which of course I was. It was simply the power of the energy that had thrown me back in time. I can't even say I felt any more than that, just a power surge so strong it reduced me to tears, but I understood the message it offered.

I quickly collected myself again and re-entered the room. There was, very conveniently, a person from the National Trust there and so I was able to ask some questions. I found out that this room was originally a hayloft. In the 1500s, it became a bedroom and then in the 1700s it was redecorated to look how it did now. So, I deduced, as the bed was not the one I saw in my regression, that I could limit the time, if I was there, to between 1500 and 1700. We then made our way to the kitchens downstairs and around the huge fireplace were hung all the coats of arms of all the kings and queens who would have visited the house. Ignoring any strange looks I may have been receiving, I got out my pendulum and went round the coats of arms to see if I could get any clarity on my time here. It didn't take long for me to reach the plaque that carried Catherine Parr's name, that Andy had heard earlier, and my pendulum began to swing wildly. It said 1543, and I was quite happy just to live in the knowledge that I had identified the period in which I lived in this beautiful house.

However, at the beginning of 2011, about eight years after the trip to Snowshill and with my life in a very different place, I was beginning to open up a whole new set of past life memories. It was February and I was at my friend Sue's house with a lovely gathering of new friends she'd recently introduced me to. I had met Sue at a voice healing weekend two years before and we had instantly made a connection and become good friends. The angel cards were out and the stories were flowing; a beautiful sharing afternoon. One member of the group was speaking of her partner who had a real fascination with Japan and was talking of going as soon as he was able. I then piped up, saying that if he couldn't get there, he should visit Snowshill Manor to see the samurai collection there.

I somehow found myself retelling my story and when I'd finished one of the girls, who is extremely knowledgeable about history as well as being an amazing astrologer, said,

"Catherine Parr died in childbirth after an abusive relationship."

Well, that kind of stopped me dead. I had always been really happy in the knowledge that I was just the lady of the manor. However, she continued to explain how Catherine was betrothed to Thomas Seymour, Jane Seymour's brother, but that when she had caught the eye of Henry VIII they were forced to put their marriage plans aside. Thomas went abroad to get his mind off her and Catherine became Henry's wife for about three years until he died. Thomas then returned, they got married and Catherine, even though this was her fourth marriage, became pregnant for the first time. But Thomas was then discovered messing around with the young Princess Elizabeth, who was only about fourteen at the time. Elizabeth was sent away out of his reach and Catherine apparently 'died of a broken heart' after the birth of her daughter Mary at Sudeley Castle. She died aged thirty-six, about the same age as this all came up for me.

I can't say it sat comfortably with me but I then became aware of a memory of my now former partner's mother producing a strange heirloom that had been passed down the family from a great-grandfather who was a Victorian vicar. In a little bundle she showed us a lock of hair and if I remember correctly, as I held it in my hands, it was still red in colour. It was allegedly the hair of one of the wives of Henry VIII. Her body was interred at a time when Andy's ancestor was able to cut himself a lock of her hair. As I was telling the girls this, I knew I didn't know which queen it was so I quickly sent a text to my ex. I was beginning to feel a little uncomfortable as too many jigsaw pieces were falling into the wrong places as far as I was concerned. I've always had a bit of an issue with people thinking they were famous people in a past life; it's an ego thing I suppose. Anyway, you can guess what came back on my phone. He had no idea of the conversation that was leading to this question, but his reply came back simply as *Catherine Parr*.

I left Sue's house with a DVD of the story of Henry VIII she happened to have, and a little more information about the queen. The following night, after watching the whole programme, I awoke with odd stomach pains and after a while I sensed this was not something I could just sleep off. I spent the next hour vomiting and through it all, I got the sense that I couldn't stomach this. Within the last month, I had received some guidance which said 'don't look back', so I decided to simply close the door behind me and continue moving forward. It didn't seem important whether I was the lady of the manor, Catherine Parr, a couple of atoms in either of their bodies or whether I am just picking up on memories held within that vast ocean of consciousness. What does seem important now is to take the knowledge we receive from such experiences and use it to heal traumas we are still holding on to deep within, to break the cycle and learn to express our emotions fully, whether they be positive or negative; they all have to come out.

For me, the blessing and the gifts that this part of our journey offers, when the sun is at its pinnacle and the moon is the ruler, are huge. We have great waves of emotions, personally, within our families and culturally, which we are suppressing to the detriment of all, especially future generations. Our children feel it most because they have not closed the door on their spiritual connections and put walls around their hearts in self-preservation, as we learn to do as adults. We can do so much for them and for ourselves by choosing to release our pain, however hard it may seem. For those of us who can dig deep to understand what is going on under our crab-like shells and go through the process of feeling and letting go of whatever it is we are holding on to, we can find contentment in the knowledge that we are showing the way for others to follow.

Although this experience only did a little to help me answer my long-asked question regarding whether or not to have children, it did help me to understand that whatever we put out into the world stems from our past, historically, genetically and emotionally. It's up to us to heal all aspects of ourselves so that we can make a positive impact on this world, whether it is through our children or those we engage with in life. The more we are willing to look within and connect with our inner feminine, the greater the understanding of ourselves we can gain to bring about the necessary healing.

Chapter 5

The Return of the King

Shine

Running with the wind, flying high,
Higher than an eagle, hear Icarus sigh.
Rising with the sun to satisfy
My hopes and yearnings, feel Isis cry.

You can shine, just hold a straight line.
Running in circles will bring you to a standstill.

So I held my breath and slowed my feet,
Until I could hear my heartbeat.
I heard it whisper like the flower from a seed,
With the sun in your heart, you're all you need.

You can shine, just hold a straight line.
Running in circles will bring you to a standstill.

We are now at the height of summer, from late July into August. The sun is strong in the sky and is beating its beautiful, golden rays upon us. Hopefully our crops have grown high and if we haven't managed to get in our garden with our secateurs and shears then it has become completely wild and overgrown. Just as, astrologically, the previous month was ruled by our moon, symbolising the mother, here we are ruled by the sun, our father. It reminds us of our royal seed, our divine inheritance. We have now travelled through all four elements: fire, earth, air and water, and now we are returning to the element of fire that we experienced in the first month. In this way, we have completed one of the smaller cycles within the many larger cycles we experience in life.

It is at this time that we find ourselves at our solar plexus, the third chakra, which is found just above the belly button and its colour is yellow. This is our energy or our power centre and it gives us our mental, conscious knowledge of ourselves. As we make that reconnection to our birth with our sun – our source, our father, at our solar centre – with a symbolic umbilical cord back home, we are remembering once more who we truly are.

We have reached adolescence on our journey around the lifetime cycle and here the mirror shows us that just like our crops, we are having that huge growth spurt, and like our garden, we are experiencing the wonderful wild exuberance of youth. Growing in confidence and prowess, we are reaching the apex of our outward growth and we can glory in our new sense of physical maturity. The fact that we are still emotionally immature creates a conflict which is highlighted particularly having stepped into the last of the three lower chakras which represent the manifest, physical duality of our life here on Earth.

We are growing ever more in our awareness of ourselves and this is developing an intensity which makes us feel increasingly self-conscious. The heightened sensitivity brings out both the shadow and the light aspects of the archetype most keenly. Appearing so confident on the outside, we are constantly preening ourselves and begin to strut our stuff on our imaginary catwalk. However, in our shadow, we become very self-obsessed, with a desperate need for approval.

Leo is the astrological archetype here and the lion beautifully represents the positives of this sign as the king of the jungle. As we bring its attributes together – this is a fire sign; its positive, masculine energy is, as I said, ruled by the sun – at our solar plexus, we rediscover the masculine, positive energy that fires our energy centre. If our conscious knowledge of who we are is strong, it is from here that we can learn to shine. Here the selfless desire to raise ourselves above the purely physical ego steps into the royal appointment for the service of others.

At this point on the astrology course I presumed I would feel right at home. I have, I discovered, a Leo ascendant. (Your ascendant is the sign that is rising on the eastern horizon at the moment of your birth; it is the aspect of yourself that you show first, your mask.) I have the hair that I wear like a mane and am very comfortable on stage doing my thing. There was, as you can imagine, so much more to discover.

At the beginning of 2008, I went to see a homeopath because a friend told me that you could be referred to one, by your doctor, on the NHS. After years of different treatments for my asthma I thought another attempt couldn't hurt. The homeopath did a very good initial consultation and I had some powder to take. However, the medicine is geared to a holistic approach to health and seemed to be directed at my energy levels, at my solar plexus. I realised this was an aspect of my condition I hadn't addressed before. If ever I got overtired I would always deflate like a blow-up doll, as if someone had pulled a plug from my belly button. Often when a healing is needed in more than one chakra, it is important to deal with the lowest first. This was certainly true for me. My heart and throat chakras, which are linked to the asthma issues, would have to wait their turn. I took the medicine and performed a lengthy Reiki healing on my solar plexus, gathering all my 'yellow' crystals together for this third chakra and third colour in the rainbow spectrum.

At the same time I was becoming aware of a link between my personal power and my voice. As we also continue our musical journey up the scale we arrive at the third note, the major third, which is also considered masculine in music.[1] Recognising I had a real weakness at my energy centre, I saw how this completely mirrored my weakness vocally as I had a big break in my voice right in the middle of my range over about four notes. This is a little unusual as most people's break is much higher. It was this break that was mainly preventing me from singing any lead vocals as it was creating a lack of confidence, and also a lack of power in my voice as the break produced a kind of dead zone in my tone quality here. It all linked into the same story. I also became aware that as the break in my voice was so large, there was more to deal with than just the solar plexus. I realised that this chakra and the heart are both central to us. In physics the third colour after red and blue (the root and higher chakras) is green, the heart chakra. In art, the third colour is yellow, the solar plexus. One is our physical energy centre and the other our emotional energy centre. Both are important in their own way and I still needed a good deal of healing in both these areas.

As soon as I took the powder I felt a shift. My lack of confidence in my personal power was also linked to my communication skills, as I would never stand up for myself in confrontational situations. There seemed to be a clear distinction for me here because in any other situation where my anger would not be aroused I would never have a problem in stating my case. I had only just learned through my regression how I stifled my anger out of fear of the monster that might appear. Now, as always, when faced with a shift in energy, a gift is immediately offered to see how you engage with the new healing received. One such situation soon came up and I felt, first of all, a memory of being momentarily back in my past life where I had chosen to opt out of life rather than face a confrontational situation. Even though the regression had occurred at least five years before, the emotion was keenly felt and I immediately understood the lesson. It was a feeling rather like a willow, being bent almost to breaking point.

I knew, however, in this life, my situation was nothing in comparison to the last; I was suffering no abuse, only needing to learn from remnants of the past life still stuck in my energetic memory. I knew I had a choice now and I chose to face my fear and face my anger and make a shift. All I had to do was lighten up. This is a message that has been offered to me many times and this time I took it. Instead of falling silent like a child who has been scolded, I threw a casual, light-hearted remark that quashed the possibility of any emotions rising out of control. It was so easy I astounded myself. I felt like I did when I was a confident young adult before I'd knocked all the confidence out of myself. I almost asked why I couldn't have done this before if it was so easy, but knew that the medicine had given me the necessary chemical rebalance to make the change.

It was this shift that brought all these new wonderful things into my life, like the amazing astrology course that I was gifted only two months later. It also gave me the strength to face my shadow, the depths of my fears. The loss of a lifetime partner, maybe many lifetimes, and the fear of being alone. I knew I was being invited on a journey.

Knowing that we had just completed the first cycle of the elements, as the day progressed I was able to examine my astrological year so far and what John's course was really offering me. I was becoming aware of the idea that we hold the energies of all the twelve archetypes within us, as we are a reflection of the whole cosmos. Just as we all live through each of the twelve months of the year, this was reminding me to connect with each energy whether I had a planet in that sign or not. In fact, the opposite was becoming true. John was expressing the idea that it was more important to connect with the signs that were not in our charts, to investigate what they had to offer. Stressing that it is really important to discover the sense of self as a whole, by engaging with what is missing in our chart we can balance the complete, uninterrupted wheel within us.

As I looked back over the previous four months, I reflected on how, in the first month, following my excitement over the immediacy of the synchronistic events that had transpired, I had written the story which I called my *Plum Tree Story* and sent it around the other members of the group. (The following year I got to tell this story at an Aries storytelling evening with the original storyteller present. This was quite a nerve-wracking experience. He, however, really enjoyed having his own story retold with a new chapter added; he said that had never happened to him before. He also threw in, in a very offhand manner, that it was never going to be a plum tree. He said the story was about a cherry tree but that he threw the plum tree in at the last minute. I nearly leapt on him. I told him it couldn't possibly be a cherry tree and when he had heard my additional part to his story, he laughed, enjoying the synchronicity he had inadvertently brought about.) I felt with this experience I had assuredly got in touch with my new creative abilities. This was the Aries spark that led to the writing of this book and all that was to come.

With Taurus, a brief look into permaculture had reminded me of our ancient herbal knowledge and I had felt a great yearning and found great joy in returning to that way of living in harmony with Mother Nature's gifts. My communication skills, unveiled in Gemini, were improving with each day. I sensed this was something I was only beginning to play with and it wouldn't be long before I would discover the bard in me. My understanding of what lessons I needed to learn in this life because of who I was, who I'd been and who had come before me was becoming clearer all the time, through my explorations in Cancer.

It's very exciting to discover you are clearly being prepared for the work that is in store and this was beginning to be true for me. One important thing that happened for me on this day on the astrology course was that for the first time, I was able to truly engage in the meditation. John had worried that I wouldn't be getting the most out of them, as I would be too busy playing the harp. This session was the first time I'd fully let go of my conscious mind whilst playing, which I had been striving to do for many years. I completely immersed myself in the very powerful meditation. To sense that I could play the harp without any conscious thought, that I could allow another, deeper, part of me take the wheel, as it were, was a very exciting place to arrive at. I realised that I had completed a journey that had taken five years to fulfil.

When I first got my harp, Louise, my crystal healer, had suggested that I didn't learn the harp technically but should just treat it as a healing tool, not get caught up in the head aspect of playing but just close my eyes and play from the heart. I heard what she said but my Saturn in Pisces decided it knew better and I couldn't resist finding a teacher, having eight months of lessons to get me started and use it to start writing my songs. Although I tried some healing, finding a teacher who gave me some tools to connect to my inner harpist, for five years I mainly concentrated on playing my songs and performing them. I soon began teaching the harp in school and I even got technical and learned how to put a songbook together on the computer and published it.

I recalled how soon after buying the harp I had a dream in which I was back playing with a band I used to play with in the early 90s. It was a Celtic/jazz band and of all the many genres I have played, the music most resembled the style I was now playing with my band, Sutura, in which I play the harp; in those days, of course, I was playing the saxophone. The only part I really remembered was that in the dream, the pianist in the band, who was blind but has now sadly died, instead of having his usual black hair, had gone grey. This kind of surprised me as I always presumed you saw people as you knew them in dreams.

As synchronicity would have it I just happened to have a clarinet pupil at the time who was a dream therapist. I asked him about this and he agreed that this was an unusual occurrence and should be acknowledged as such. He then proceeded to tell me about a book he thought I should read. It was called *Turlough* by Brian Keenan, one of the hostages in Lebanon, written about the life of Turlough O'Carolan, the 17th century blind Irish harper. The book was wonderful and the story that led him to write it is also a poignant tale of how he believed Turlough, coming to him as a dream-walker, helped him through the ordeal of four years in captivity. He wrote the book to honour this fact, although he also took some prodding to get there. But I realised I was being prompted by a blind pianist and a blind harpist to close my eyes and play as if I were blind. However, it was a gift I found difficult to take on and it soon slipped from my regime.

Here I was five years later, finally honouring the gift myself. I had been, in fact, 'trying' too hard, as usual, and when I finally let go of trying with my head and stepped into my heart it was as easy as riding a bike. I recalled that the teacher who had given me the healing tools had told me to connect to my higher self through my solar plexus. The mental energy that we hold here is connected to our core, a powerful and deep essence of ourselves. We have a core beat if you can feel and listen closely. Here we can lock into our psychic abilities and just feel our way. I really only needed to remember to play without my eyes, but with insight. It is when we go within that we really start to sense how brightly we shine.

Although the Leo archetype is one of inner contentment and can be quite inactive, it was becoming apparent, as I became aware of the landscape zodiacs that were being discovered, that the gateway to finding them was always through the Leo sign.[2] Many landscape zodiacs, it seemed, began with the discovery of the Leo formation. It seemed as if the lion sat at the doorway as you stepped in, like the great stone lions at the bottom of the driveway to a stately home. This is the extrovert side of Leo, the showman who loves to strut his or her stuff on the stage. As my ascendant is Leo and this is the quality that steps into the room first, I soon became aware of how this was also working for me. As a musician I have always felt comfortable on stage and when I joined the ten-piece party band in 1992, dressing up and putting on a big show was all part of an act that suited me to the ground (both Seb and Andy were already members before I joined), but here I was being invited to go much deeper. My album with my own band Sutura, put together in 2007, before I had learned anything about astrology, opens with my Leo song *Shine*. When John put some of my music on his website he chose the song *Shine* to open the film footage. It seemed I was being given no option but to shine; no more hiding from my true purpose.

In my performance I talk about arriving at the solar plexus and learning that if our knowledge of self is strong then we can be humble in that power we hold. The problems begin when our lower chakras are closed; we are holding on to fear in our root chakra and feeling disconnected to our world around us in our sacral chakra. So we arrive at our solar plexus and our knowledge of self is weak. Then we feel the need to steal power from or overpower others. My song *Shine* was actually inspired by the words of Marianne Williamson, which Nelson Mandela used in his inauguration speech, where she says that not only do we have the right to shine but the duty to shine, for in shining ourselves we allow those around us to also shine.[3] As an English person, I sense that we have quite an issue with fulfilling this. Words and phrases such as 'arrogant' and 'blowing our own trumpet' create a culture of frowning on those who truly step into their own light; there can be a fine line between humility and hiding yourself under a bushel and arrogance and shining. I believe it is time for us to let go of our fears of discovering who we truly are and what we are really capable of and allow ourselves to shine without reticence. When we can all learn to shine with confidence, we remove the power struggle and will naturally find a sense of humility.

The path we take in Leo, where we are reminded of our divine heritage, is called the hero's journey. From the age of eighteen to thirty, the heroes disappear from our stories to find themselves and become men. We see it in all the heroic stories and films, from Jesus' life to Superman, Luke Skywalker in *Star Wars*; the list goes on. The hero has a time in his or her life when they go into hiding to rediscover themselves so they can follow their destiny, fight their demons and find their power. As John explained this I felt my whole body shake with the intensity of what I was feeling. I had been experiencing my time of hiding and now I was preparing to do the work so that I could re-emerge, like the butterfly from the cocoon. This is everyman's story but I seemed to be experiencing it right now.

An image that has stayed with me for some time and has recently come up in conversation more and more is an amalgamation of two scenes in the Peter Jackson adaptation of *The Fellowship of the Ring*[4] when the hobbit, Bilbo Baggins, is just leaving after his disappearing act at his party. As he is attempting to leave the ring for Frodo, his attachment to it is clear when he gets annoyed with the wizard, Gandalf, for pointing this out. He tries to cover this up by claiming that he believes Gandalf wants it for himself. What happens next is a wonderful piece of cinematography and resonated strongly with me. Gandalf seems to double in stature in a very powerful and almost frightening way and orders Bilbo not to take him for a conjurer of cheap tricks. Later, when Gandalf returns to Frodo and explains what power the ring holds, Frodo becomes very scared and immediately tries to give the ring back to Gandalf. He then asks Frodo not to tempt him, for he doesn't dare take it, not even purely for the safety of the ring. He tries to explain that he would use the ring from a desire of wanting to do good, but that, through him, it could wield a power too great and terrible to imagine.

Having not seen this film for a few years my memory had fused these two scenes together. I remembered the part where Gandalf doubled in stature with the words he said to Frodo, and when I spoke of this to others no one picked me up on it. It seemed more important that the energy was telling me what I needed to hear: that we all fear the huge power we hold. Indeed, I could see that all the main characters, Frodo, Gandalf and of course Aragorn, shy away from their destinies and great powers only to finally discover them through their own hero's journey and come out shining.

Shying away from our destiny is something we can all relate to. The more I looked into our reasons to choose not to shine, the more I kept coming up with the idea that there is great fear in the amount of power we actually have at our fingertips. I had heard that atom for atom we actually contain more potential energy than the sun. When I failed to find the source of this fact I was synchronistically introduced to a quantum physicist who assured me this was correct. Bill Bryson, in his *A Short History of Nearly Everything*, says:

If you are an average-sized adult you will contain within your modest frame no less than 7×10^{18} joules of potential energy – enough to explode with the force of thirty very large hydrogen bombs.[5]

As we begin to discover how immensely powerful we truly are, we realise the havoc that the misuse of this power can create. This can seem frightening, especially for men – I am, of course, generalising here – as the masculine energy is more outward, whereas the feminine energy is more encircling, but also, I believe, because there is a sense that this misuse has happened before. The fear that this brings up for us enables us to block the knowledge of it, like a child blocking the memory of a trauma. This concept, I realised, held a lot of truth for myself as well as for others I spoke to and, inspired by the words in an email I received, I put it into a song. The lyrics go:

We help the child who fears the night but who helps those who fear the light?

This is something we need to address. But I think it is something we can work towards with a lightness of heart rather than a heavy one. It is time to choose the light and there is nothing more joyful than learning to shine so that you can inspire someone else to reflect that right back at you.

It is with great joy, and I am aware that many others are finding themselves in similar place, that although it has taken me many years I am finally able to stand up and say that I believe that the work I do is good. Although I have been involved in many wonderful musical projects over the years as a saxophonist, I never felt comfortable listening to myself or felt I was a worthy member. Now I work mostly alone with my harp, so there is only me to judge or not judge and although I know I still have a long way to go I am thoroughly happy with what I do. For those who also find themselves in this place it's a feeling that constantly surprises me in the nicest way. I remember feeling, as a young adult, before my awakening, that there must be something more I had to offer, that my life as a saxophonist/teacher couldn't be it. Though I was right, I didn't really imagine it possible at the time. Yet when John showed me how my chart revealed that my healing work would take time to find its way in my lifetime journey, it all made sense.

So much of this reticence to shine comes from judgement and it is such a powerful aspect of ourselves that we have forgotten how much it pervades all that we do. Feeling that we ourselves are judged, as many religions tell us that God will judge us when we leave this world, we have been held in this state of fear for millennia now. There are many that no longer feel this is right, and Neale Donald Walsch, in his book *Communion with God*, helped me understand this. This has come from our understanding that religion teaches us that God is separate from us, so we have a need to return to God. The fact that we might not be allowed back into his kingdom keeps us in fear; the fact that we never left is kept from us. In believing that we are constantly being judged, we then turn this most powerful judgement on to ourselves. Being so adept at judging, we naturally become very quick to judge others. The fact that our prisons are now full to bursting reflects this.

It is becoming clearer day by day that there is another way. Using the hero's journey to understand our own story, our own reason for being, is at the heart of solving these issues and as I learn how to remove judgement of myself I find it easier not to judge others, but to choose to see their pain. Most violent acts are committed as violence against the self projected out into the world. Imprisonment just fulfils this belief of being judged and will never heal the problem. I believe there are better ways of helping those that have acted out their pain on others. Journeying, self-realisation and a good deal of empathy and healing are needed so that we can offer them a true awareness of themselves, and release them from their pain so that they can step back into society on a new path and with a healed heart. I know this is a dream but I also know that it has already begun to find its way into our society in the form of restorative justice, and is not only possible but absolutely necessary. This new understanding simply creates a desire, even an imperative, for me to slow my pace of life so I can see the world for all the light and beauty it holds. I trust that you and many others are feeling the same.

On our astrology day John explained the link between the fire signs. He said that Aries is the spark as it creates the fire and Leo tends the fire. This is why Leos can also be seen as lazy; they are content to sit and watch over the fire that has been created, quietly and inwardly shining. Only when we learn to do this will we be ready to spread the fire in Sagittarius.

Learning that we are now entering the Age of Aquarius (which is all about community), and that Aquarius has Leo as its opposition (facing each other as they sit at opposite sides of the wheel), I realised that humanity has to make steps to heal the individual before we can raise the vibration of the whole. As the few start to really shine the flames will spread like wildfire.

Following in my father's footsteps, I have never really pushed myself. There has always been a quest for contentment over financial or career success. I have never had a full-time job and I am very protective of my time to think and be creative. When I looked up my Mayan astrology last year it said I was a yellow sun, and that I need time and space in my life to fulfil my spiritual quest. This abated any fears I had of not fulfilling certain social goals. As I have now ceased judging myself and stopped using words such as 'lazy' or 'arrogant' about myself as I feel these are society's words, I think my life has gained more worth since I have had time to examine it and understand myself. I somehow feel we would do well as a community to spend a little more time tending our fires and contemplating where our next step forward would be best placed, rather than stampeding onwards without thought in a state of fear and panic. A slower pace of life and a more contented way of being would probably suit most of us. For me, I wouldn't want it any other way.

Chapter 6

Reap What You Sow

The Wanderer

I met a man along the road; he said he was a wanderer.
He helped me with my heavy load and I told him of my life.
He was a kindly soul and offered words of wisdom,
But I couldn't take it all, I thought, what could he know?
Then he looked into my eyes and I saw my life reflected.
Like an atom magnified, it was a part of the whole.

We are the embodiment of man, reach in if you can.
We have one life, one goal, one heart and one soul.
We are the embodiment of man, reach in if you can.

He said, "If you only see the skin you see the prisoner within,
"If you look into their eyes, you see their soul realised.
"If you look into their soul, you feel the love unfold.
"If you hold on to the love you set the prisoner free."
Then he took a stick and drew a figure in the dusty road
And in my heart I knew it was a vision of his world.

We are the hands, the people who work and toil the land.

We are the head, the thinkers who help us understand.
We are the feet, the travellers that show us the way.
We are the heart, so let love have its say.

Who are you forsaking, when you try to stand alone?
Whose heart are you breaking? No one's but your own.

We are the embodiment of man, reach in if you can.
We have one life, one goal, one heart and one soul.
We are the embodiment of man, reach in if you can.
We have one life, one goal, one heart and one soul.
We are the embodiment of man, reach in if you can.

And just like that, the end of summer is in sight. In this month, from late August through September, the days are getting shorter and the nights are getting cooler. The crops have reached the end of their journey in the soil and it is time to bring in the harvest, to gather the fruits of our labours and reap our rewards to prepare for the months ahead. It is with immense joy that we need to get back in touch with Mother Earth and be prepared to get our hands dirty. Reflecting this, A. T. Mann shows us that our childhood is now coming to an end. As we get out in the fields with our sickle and scythe and cut back that wild exuberance of youth, we are preparing for adulthood in the same way that we are preparing to last out the second half of our journey as Mother Earth begins her time of breathing in and winter approaches. It is time to acknowledge our sense of achievement here, our pride in what we have accomplished and our gratitude for the gifts we receive and therefore can give.

By the time we had reached the Virgo weekend of my astrology course, I felt really in the flow of it all. The group was becoming far more cohesive, with deepening friendships and trust. With the Leo energy, the lord of his domain, we had all got in touch and reconnected with our divinity, our royal inheritance. During the day we had had great fun preening ourselves and stroking our tails. We had gone from deep meditation to role play, and for the grand finale we walked the red carpet and were regally crowned.

However, as we entered Virgo we sensed the party was over. Virgo is an earth sign once more, a feminine, receptive energy, hence our need to reconnect with Mother Earth for this time of harvesting. It is also the sign of the virgin. The sexual potency that we all carry in adolescence is waiting to blossom. The emotions within us, the rollercoaster cocktail of hormones coursing through our bodies at this time, are not to be underestimated. Like a volcano waiting to erupt, it is really important to travel through these unchartered territories with care. There are many paths on the road to sexual maturity. If it is nurtured with love and a feeling of security and inner self-realisation then future relationships will be developed with stability and kindness. If we are taught that we are sinners for wanting to enjoy the pleasures of sex then the journey begins with feelings of guilt, shame and confusion. We can find ourselves in dark places when faced with such intimate relations and it is important to recognise the healing that is needed for our society to have a positive relationship with sex. Guiding our youths through this time with a healthy and happy attitude to the experiences they are going to face is surely something we all feel is important.

At this point in the year, Greek mythology offers the story of Persephone. She is the daughter of Demeter, the goddess of the harvest, who is abducted by Hades, or Pluto, god of the underworld. Here we see the maiden brought into sexual maturity and her life of service to humanity, as queen of the underworld, gifts us the seasonal cycles. She is always shown with a sheaf of corn. This symbolic loss of childhood, growing up both physically and spiritually, embracing the light and the shadow, is a vital initiation. To be able to step into adulthood fully and remove the wheat from the chaff is important for all humanity. Without the stories and necessary wisdom passed down from the elders we have lost the customs and practices that teach us how to let go of the childhood mindset, harvesting all we have gleaned from our youth, and become fully grown adults. The introduction of the underworld is important as we begin to touch on the concept of our fear of death. Starting to embrace this idea here will help us on our journey as we grow up.

In the same light, we are discovering, at this time, the vast potential of our own unique talent that is ours to be revealed and put out into the big wide world. We are entering the time of the apprenticeship or university. Virgo is also the sign of the worker. Here we realise that though we are king of our own domain in Leo, we are also just a working cell in the body of the human race. We are both the king and the peasant, the managing director and the secretary. It is up to us to unveil what we have to offer that will heal ourselves and heal our place in that body, our world. Now considered to be ruled by Chiron, the wounded healer asteroid, Virgo is the sign of the healer, of life in servitude. This archetype reminds us of our deepest wound, the knowledge that we are all going to die. This notion brings us back down to earth with a bump, but when we free ourselves of the fear, it allows us to let go of our ego and step into a greater sense of who we really are; where we discover that death is just part of the illusion.

It is at this point that the healing brings the understanding that servitude is not something to run away from but to run towards with open arms as it will bring to us our greatest joy and purpose. To give is to receive, they are one action, and whether it's in the form of the menial, daily task or an amazing discovery, each is highly valuable. A vital lesson that the Leo king has to learn, as part of the initiation into adulthood, is humility.

Contemplating our life purpose is something we all tend

to do at different points in our lives. With my awakening in 1998, I thought about my own work as a saxophonist and music teacher and where it was leading me. Often, it only takes a few nudges to encourage us to try a new route. My first, I believe, was somewhat extraordinary. A year after Seb had awakened me and filled my life with new experiences that would sometimes leave me brimming with tears of joy at the pure beauty of it all, she left for Los Angeles. The next five months seemed strangely empty. However, in July 2000, Emma, also from the big party band, returned from a short leave of absence she had taken to integrate her own awakening. She immediately introduced me to her pendulum and then her sister-in-law, Louise, two months later. Emma rapidly became my mentor in Seb's absence.

She told me she had been doing something that she called 'sound channelling'. I had no idea what this was, but I and another singer from the same band thought it might be worth a go and maybe a bit of a laugh. I had no idea what I was letting myself in for. We arrived at Emma's terraced house and went upstairs into her spare bedroom. She told us to open our mouths, create an initial sound and then let any energy present take over. We were sitting at three separate points around a small table and then Emma said she sensed a few light beings in the room. They were behind me, she said, and as I turned around to look, although I saw nothing, I suddenly heard a huge resonance, like a massive vibration behind my left ear. It was so loud and so surprising I leapt out of my seat only to look at the two girls and realise they had heard nothing. As they confirmed this, I was beginning to feel a little spooked. I asked if these light beings were using this sound to ask me to move as I obviously had my back to them. Without waiting for an answer I changed my seat to one without my back to that wall.

As we began to sing, or rather wail, the sounds coming out of our mouths were swooping and sliding from high to low, and though we had no idea what was coming next we were often amazed how we would suddenly be sounding in unison, covering huge ranges of pitch. It was like a vocal rollercoaster and every time we paused for breath we'd dissolve into fits of laughter, although the experience was also very powerful. Emma then received some information from 'upstairs' that there were not just a half-dozen light beings sharing our performance, but a whole host of them. I suddenly got the sense that we were in a huge, rectangular auditorium with grand pillars down each side, like being in ancient Greece. The scene was bathed in wonderful hues of soft pinks, blues and gold. A heavenly order? No wonder they wanted me to move if I had my back to all that. Meanwhile, it was getting late and Emma's partner returned home and went to bed in the next room. We carried on for a little while, even though we were making a huge racket. I presumed Emma had very tolerant neighbours. Then, energised by this amazing experience, we offered our thanks and called it a night.

The next day, Emma called us both to tell us that after we'd gone and she'd gone to bed, she had begun to apologise to her partner about the noise. He looked at her with surprise and said that he had heard lots of giggling but none of the whooping or wailing that she was describing. We were all absolutely astounded. How could he not have heard all that?

Important as it is to know one's field of practice, I have since done a little research into the world of higher dimensions but as yet I have never experienced anything quite like that, where there seemed to be an actual physical shift from one to the next. I will, of course, keep searching to repeat the experience and for the technical explanation of what happened. Both are like Holy Grails to me, as I still find it difficult to fully believe what I am writing here. But following my first dip, I was well and truly hooked. I was also excited by the fact that I had had an aural experience in the form of the resonance

I had heard. It was this experience that sent me very firmly on my way into sound healing and I have used this practice through all the years that followed.

After this unusual first plunge into the world behind the veil, I began to develop a deeper understanding of the nature of sound and vibration. Bringing it into my performance work as a saxophonist seemed inevitable, but it would soon become the whole purpose of my work as singer/songwriter and harpist.

It seems to be that once we embark on this new way of seeing the universe, knowing that everything in our world is vibration, becoming a healer can feel very important as it's something we can all do; we just have to believe it is possible. The role of the healer is to simply be present, help channel the energy needed and witness the receiver's desire to be healed. In this sense we are all healers at all times and love is the only required qualification. When we truly know that in giving we are receiving at the same time, then we can all begin to embrace the role of the healer as something that we simply are. Taking away the mysticism, I believe, can be very helpful.

For many, life in servitude can be about discovering why we are here and what we can offer the world when we are at our best. Finding our way out of a job that makes us deeply unhappy, so that we can follow our dreams, is not always easy but if we can begin the process towards making changes in our lives then often the universe will step in to ease the transition. While we are a long way from having even the majority of people being able to offer the world what they are here to give, I feel it is imperative that those lucky enough to find what their role is should step into it without hesitation. There is a huge sense of contentment and achievement that comes with this and, for people like me, it is important not to feel guilt here, just humility and gratitude.

Healing kind of fell into my lap; pendulums and crystals

just seemed to follow naturally and at our first meeting, Louise, the crystal healer, gifted me with a very simple healing method. She told me to simply point to three places on the receiver's body: beneath their feet at the earth star chakra, their heart, and above their head at the soul star chakra. As I pointed to each chakra I was told to sing a note that felt appropriate with the understanding that there was no 'wrong' note, but that I should just trust. I was given some simple blessings and signs to offer, but anyone wishing to try this should trust whatever they feel guided to do as long as they ask that it be done in the highest good. This all seemed fairly straight-forward enough even for me, a novice.

During this one visit, Louise downloaded a huge amount of information for me and I left for America to visit Seb in LA three days later with my head reeling. We hadn't seen each other for eight months and at the end of my second night there, after hours of catching up, Seb told me she was holding on to a huge amount of pain that was shooting down her right arm and now was beginning to climb up into her neck and head. She said it had been bothering her for ten days.

Within a few minutes I became aware of a pain in my right shoulder and sensed it wasn't my pain, but was perhaps a little nudge for me to try out my new healing technique. I went over to where she was sitting and touched the equivalent point on her shoulder where I could feel this twinge I was sensing. I asked her if this was the point that hurt most for her. She agreed that it was there, thinking it was a trapped nerve. I told her what I had been shown and suggested that perhaps this was a gift and that I should try it out on her. Seb was happy to oblige and so I went through the procedure and took my first virgin solo flight as a healer. Of course, even as I write this, I know that we are all healing beings and have the opportunity to be healed and heal ourselves in every moment, but I suppose I mean this was the first prescribed healing, with facilitator and receiver in full knowledge of what was occurring. Remembering what Louise had told me, I tentatively sang the notes, starting low in pitch and raising it each time, directing them to the three points below, at the centre and above her body. It felt strange singing to a singer, though I knew this was nothing to do with the quality of my singing voice and was all about intention. Not really knowing what my best was, I had a damn good go at it anyway and hoped it was good enough. When I had finished we both felt it had been a long day, so turned in for the night.

When she awoke the next morning the pain had completely gone. I was completely astounded and I think Seb was pretty surprised too as she'd been carrying it for quite a while. Mostly, I was excited to think that just singing three notes could have such an effect.

As all those who are blessed to work with this energy will agree, the journey is always a beautiful one, but as I have said, I feel the most important healing work anyone can do is on themselves. My family has always been open to alternative therapies and all through my twenties I continued to try every type of alternative healing I was drawn to. I was born with eczema, which turned to asthma at the age of twenty-six. A few years after I was diagnosed with asthma an acupuncturist actually cured it for nearly a year. I then moved into a dusty, derelict house that Andy and I renovated over a few years, my acupuncturist left the city and suddenly it all came back again.

When I met Louise in 2000, at the age of thirty-four, she also gave me some breathing exercises with light, which I called my Auric Boundary exercise. With this new daily practice, for almost a year my asthma seemed cured again, only to return eight months later, after my regression. This had peeled back another layer and exposed more work to be done. I kept trying whatever other alternative therapies came along that resonated with me, but it seemed to be becoming more important to understand the reason why I had contracted it in the first place, before the long-term healing could take place. The months of being asthma-free were, for me, messages to let me know that it was curable, but only after the root of the issue was healed. A simple analogy is one of light bulbs working in series, understanding that it is important to discover and heal the first experience of trauma, otherwise you could be forever sifting through your many journeys, which are all just repeats of the first. Turn off this light; get to the core and all the lights go off in one fell swoop. However, I still had to wait for some missing pieces of the jigsaw. It took another two years from this point in the astrology course, in Virgo, for the necessary information to begin to unfold like a rose that slowly unfurls its petals.

By the end of 2008, time seemed to be speeding up for me and I felt like I was on a fast-moving conveyer belt. A wonderful job opportunity, the details of which I will go into later, took me back to my old synagogue that I hadn't stepped inside for thirty years. This brought back memories of my wonderful childhood, but reminded me of my rabbi, a survivor of the Holocaust, and the huge sense of empathy I had for him and others less fortunate than myself. This developed in me my strong sense of guilt, which is held collectively, but not exclusively, by Jews as a race.

Within a month of revisiting my synagogue, in July 2009 I was guided to attend a healing course. It was called ThetaHealing and deals with information we store at a cellular level, individually, genetically and at the soul level. I learned that, like crystals, our cells carry memory and hold on to thought beliefs. Our conscious thoughts are just the tip of the iceberg, just our ego communicating itself to the world, but below the surface we have all our subconscious thoughts, our dream state consciousness. Beneath this again are thought programmes which have been passed down through our ancestry in our genetic coding, from the egg cell from our mother, combining with the sperm cell of our father. Those first cells divide again and again to make up who we are, and contain all the beliefs of our parents and their parents before them and so on. Theta Healing helps us to remove any of these deep-seated damaging beliefs we may be holding on to and replace them with positive and beneficial ones. This was very profound, and of course very synchronistic.

I looked back at how this all reflected on my life on a physical level. My eczema had stayed with me through childhood, until I was twenty-one, and at the age of twenty-five, I suffered a couple of bad viral colds. The following year I was diagnosed with asthma. I had always blamed the fact that doctors had given me steroids to heal my eczema as a child. Thinking it was curing it, as a teenager, I was unaware that the steroids just suppressed the symptoms only for them to reveal themselves later as asthma. However, I needed to take some responsibility here.

The more we learn about our journey and healing, the more we begin to understand that, as everything is a reflection of itself, physical symptoms are just a mirror of the energetic aspects of ourselves that need to be healed in our aura. If we revisit the concept of the Russian doll idea and the holographic principle then our body is just a manifestation of everything we hold in our aura, whether it is revealed as an aspect of beauty or pain. Our aura is made up of light and sound, which is vibration, and vibration contains information and wisdom. The spectrum of frequency waves is vast and we have harnessed many of these already, for instance, radio waves bringing information into our homes. However, the vibrations held in our emotional body are energetic, which are all about feeling. Unfortunately, when we get caught up in the facts and figures of these vibrations we often lose sight of how to heal. We forget about the emotional aspect and just concentrate on the formulas and chemistry, only looking at the physical body. This leads to a heavy reliance on pills instead of working with the healing energy of love and forgiveness held in our aura. I knew a broader view was needed.

Until this point, I held an idea of seeing our lives, metaphorically, as a painting that had been whitewashed over; we have to gradually clean away the whitewash to uncover the picture below and so understand our history. Only when the full picture is visible can we have the true understanding of how to heal it completely. I had conceived this image after seeing a programme on television about paintings that were being discovered in crypts of churches that had been hidden away rather than being destroyed during the beginning of our five-hundred-year journey away from our spiritual freedom. One such painting was about to be thrown away as it seemed to be just a piece of white board, when someone noticed something and began investigating further. What they discovered was a rare piece of our history, most of which has been lost. However, although these are wonderful stories about discovering our artistic heritage, I soon realised that a better analogy of our healing journey is that of the mirror that has to be cleaned to reveal the true reflection.

Over the years, with all the many different types of healing we can investigate, I believed I was gaining a deeper insight into what had caused my asthma. Unexpressed grief is one of the main causes which I had discovered from my past life regression, and I was realising that guilt was also a probable contributor. I had searched my personal history, I thought quite extensively, trying to establish what had triggered the asthma to come at that time. It took seventeen years, until this moment in 2009, for me to put two and two together to realise that it started when I moved into my first house in 1992. This was made possible after I inherited a sum of money which came to me via my mother following the death of my maternal grandmother.

With my two older sisters already on the property ladder, my parents decided they would be happier to see me settled now and my sisters would get their share later. At the time I was very conscious of the responsibility, how indebted I felt and how much extra guilt I might be piling on myself. However, I was soon to discover that there was more than the receipt of my house that led to the onset of my asthma. It was clear to me that guilt alone wasn't a strong enough cause for such a powerful shift in my breathing issues. However, I was going to have to wait another year for the rest of the picture to fully reveal itself. In the summer of 2010, I met, very synchronistically, a wonderful Dutch lady called Johanna. She soon became a good friend and not only did she help me get my writing to flow, she also gave me this much-needed last piece of the jigsaw.

One day, as I was telling Johanna the history of my asthma and explaining how I felt I had begun to heal it, she responded by saying,

"Oh, I thought that asthma came through the mother. I have a friend whose daughter has asthma and they have come to this understanding of it."

I was surprised, as I knew I had no issues with my mother that would bring about this kind of journey. Then I stopped dead in my tracks; something I had not thought about for nearly twenty years. I remembered, after my grandma's funeral, my mother saying how she had sat down for the first time and talked openly with her siblings. They all discussed their mother's difficulty with showing her love and my mum in particular had felt unloved by her mother. Coupled with the knowledge that they had been evacuated during the war when the youngest was four years old, I remember feeling shocked to the core by this at the time. As I recalled this so many years later with my new friend I felt that tightening in my chest once more. My empathy doesn't let me get away with anything and this gripped me hard. As I let the memory sit with me for a few moments, I realised that the asthma began here as I took on my mother's pain. When I received the money for my house from my grandma, I realised that as the money was skipping the generation, then so was the asthma. As I talked this through with Johanna we were amazed at the clarity of the situation and I felt very honoured that I had obviously chosen, on a higher level of course, to take this on, perhaps in the knowledge that I would be able to heal it, even if it would take nineteen years.

The ThetaHealing course helped me to remove many of my damaging thought beliefs held in my cellular make-up, but I was only just beginning to work with this energy. I had created a shift, loosened the mortar, but my asthma was very deep-seated and I knew at the time it was going to take quite a bit more investigation and all-round hard work to heal my breathing problems in my heart chakra.

In August 2010, John Wadsworth, the astrologer and creator of the Alchemical Journey, invited me to meet with a group of fascinating people, all connected by their passion for the Glastonbury Zodiac. This is a discovery that the landscape can contain a mirror of the constellations of the zodiac; as above, so below. On the last day of the astrological Grand Cross alignment, when all the outer planets were held in a great cross in the sky, we journeyed together to the centre of the Glastonbury Zodiac in Park Wood. Globally and personally, it was a pivotal moment. Here I was in the Glastonbury Zodiac, at its heart, aware that the last piece in my jigsaw puzzle that I needed to manifest began with the need to heal my heart. Here, I could feel my whole life journey, from my head to my heart: from an atheist to finding my spiritual journey, from studying the technical world of the saxophone, to the healing world of the harp. I sensed as I was reconnecting with the land and with so many amazing people who were all absorbing themselves in their own journeying that there was much to learn here. We were discovering stories old and new, walking the land and listening to its song – it felt like a real homecoming.

This meeting was also pivotal in bringing this book together, although it began in small increments, which would play a part in my healing. The group was already in the process of putting together a compilation of ideas about the Glastonbury Zodiac; whether it was a technical essay or a poem, everyone was taking part. As I watched everyone in the group hand their work to Celia Gunn, an author and part co-ordinator of the project, I wondered whether I might be able to be a part of it. At lunch I brought up the subject with her, intimating that as I felt I was here very synchronistically (John had invited me at the last minute, asking me to bring my harp. When we arrived, the original musician who was meant to play hadn't shown up, so I seamlessly filled the gap), that maybe I could be involved. I explained that I had written a book; this book in its first incarnation. Although Celia acknowledged the synchronicity of events, she reminded me that any article had to be about the zodiac. I searched through my chapters to find a thread I could piece together especially for this compilation book. It wasn't long before the whole piece took shape – starting with the story where I walk the Aquarius figure in Chapter 11 – and then began to have a life of its own.

That summer brought my seventeen-year relationship to a close. It was with much sadness but also a huge amount of love that I was beginning to be able to let go. The following month brought us into Virgo, the virgin – potentiality – and it was at this time that I met another amazing man. Feeling a huge connection, I instigated a first date. It was a very short connection, as the timing simply wasn't right and, with great wisdom, my new friend stepped out of the ring, sensing that he wasn't ready for what I was offering. However, in that short amount of time we had two powerful moments of intimacy. After the first I felt a huge shift in my heart chakra, which seemed to cause many people to comment on how much stronger my singing voice was. Following the second I had an asthma attack at night, and instead of having to fight my breathing patterns, my lungs let go with ease. It seemed as if the attack was brought on just to show me the healing that had occurred. The healing was profound and the asthma still didn't return, even through the coldest winter I can remember, which normally can be a real struggle for me. It was an amazing revelation that my asthma could be healed in such a simple way, a pure gift from the heart, and giving me my fourth, and I hoped final, respite from this ailment I had suffered from for so long.

A month or so later, I was again invited to join some friends from the Glastonbury Zodiac group, Tim and Sophie, on a walk back into the heart of the Glastonbury Zodiac in Park Wood. I suddenly remembered that it was the 12th of December; the anniversary of what would have been an eighteen-year relationship had my ex and I made it this far. I was being offered a chance to process some more letting go and the land and its wisdom gave me that chance once again. My heart was now strong enough to do this with love, enough for Andy and myself.

I had completed my piece for the compilation book about the Glastonbury Zodiac back in September but it had seemed at the time that it wasn't finished. When I sent it to Celia she said not to worry, it could wait till January. I relaxed, sensing that maybe something might happen to give the story a proper ending. As I reached this point in December, I realised how the experience of writing the piece had actually been instrumental in helping to tie the story together, working alongside the amazing resolutions I had received with the healing of my asthma and my long-term relationship. Or was it the zodiac energy that, in two transformative visits, had brought the necessary healing in such a joyful way?

Life in servitude is a huge concept, one that in our Western culture we find hard to conceive. It reminds us of Victorian

Britain, when many were living like slaves to the wealthy. However, although this is still true for most of us, this is an outdated story. I believe it is up to us to recognise that the more we find our own happiness and heal the issues that are embedded deep in our beings, the easier we can step into the true sense of this role. If we can begin with ourselves, as this is the only place we can truly make a change, we can equip ourselves with the necessary tools to offer our unique gifts to the world and begin to grow as individuals and so as a community. The amazing sense of fulfilment we receive as we give knows no bounds and can only be understood when we accept the position with all our heart.

The more we can do to heal ourselves as we journey, the more we raise the healing vibration within our own bodies. It is this higher vibration that we then offer to others. Cleaning the mirror is a job that never ends and becomes part of the joy of our work here. I have certainly found great pleasure in rolling up my sleeves, getting my hands dirty and harvesting Mother Nature's wisdom in order to see things more clearly. We can now start to bring all our stories together with all the wisdom they offer and put them in a huge melting pot with our new understanding of how to move forward. I believe we can start listening to ourselves and the land on which we live, in ways that have long been forgotten, so that we can fully heal our wounds and grow.

There's nothing like viewing a particular sequence of events in your life to see how everything suddenly makes sense. The light bulb moments are sublime even though some take a while to come on. But I was feeling that I was at last on my way and had passed the apprenticeship, working through the six stages of youth to step into a spiritual adulthood, gaining the potential to step forward with my newfound strength and my heart open. We have carried the pain of the wounded healer energy for long enough and now it's time to graduate and climb on to the next rung on the ladder.

Chapter 7

The Golden Mirror

Sutura

This prayer tattooed on my heart, is my sutura,
Makes my love purer.
This moment's all I know is true, makes my intention
A clear reflection of you.

And it's beautiful all the way, beautiful in every way.

You are my shining star, you hold me tighter
And I shine brighter.
We are a living déjà vu, reflecting in each face
All the love and truth and grace of you.

And it's beautiful all the way, beautiful in every way.
And it's beautiful all the way, beautiful in every way.

And it's through you I find love
And it's through you I show my love, we are love.

And it's beautiful all the way, beautiful in every way.
And it's beautiful all the way, beautiful in every way.

This prayer tattooed on my heart, is my sutura
Makes my love purer.
You know that we can only win.
It's a chocolate box selection, the joy of connection. Breathe in.

And it's beautiful all the way, beautiful in every way.
And it's beautiful all the way, beautiful in every way.

The leaves are turning and autumn is upon us. They are going from green to red, from the heart chakra back through the chakra colours to the root, returning to source. Some say it is the most beautiful time of the year, and we are now stepping into adulthood up until the age of forty-two. We are now not just learning to live but also learning to die, but it is beautiful. It is this journey towards death as we step into autumn that we have been preparing for in our apprenticeship in the previous stage on our journey. We are now at the Autumn Equinox, the 21st of September, and for the first time we can stand at this place at the midway point and look back to the start of our journey at the Spring Equinox and see our first opposition, our first reflection. After all the 'me, me, me' of youth and school and learning, we can now step into adulthood, into our heart chakra and with a true understanding of love, look at that reflection and say, "Ah, you." For me, the whole concept of this time of growing up and becoming mature adults, having completed all the initiations of childhood, is about love. The 'beingness' of love is so fundamental to who and what we are, and if we have forgotten this then the return to remembering is our soul purpose.

To help us on our way, a beautiful image on which we can reflect is the solar eclipse. It reminds us that our journey is all about that symbolic conjunction as the sun and moon engage in this beautiful cosmic union. The sun and moon, being symbolic of the father and the mother, coming together to produce this amazing diamond ring effect, gives us the wonderful embrace of the masculine and feminine; representing the marriage. Here we are being presented with one of the true wonders of our exceptional time here on Earth. The fact that they appear exactly the same size in the sky though the actual sizes and distances are so vastly different cannot, in my mind, be put down to coincidence. It feels as if it is proof of the numerical and physical perfection of the timing of our existence on Earth. It is part of the equation of life, especially as it is for a limited time only as the moon will gradually move further away from the Earth and in a few million years we shall lose this phenomenon.

Now marriage has become a very important part of our culture, but an interesting man, Bruno Bettelheim, in his book *Uses of Enchantment*, which I read over twenty years ago, taught me that our fairy tales, handed down to us through the ages, which end in marriage, are not actually about the marriage between two people but the marriage of the energy within each of us, the balance of the masculine and feminine; the way to the golden city.

It is this sacred union, that lies deep in our hearts, that is the reflection of all that is, and this 'all that is' is love; love at its highest state of being. Call it God, call it the universe, call it what you will, but it lies within us all. The closest we get to it with words is 'unconditional love', but how many of us know what that truly is? The idea of utopia is to fully grasp the utmost clarity of what that means; loving without conditions and working through the necessary healing so we can forgive without question and find peace in our hearts.

Like the Christians have the cross, the Star of David is now recognised to be the symbol used by the Jews. It is a six-pointed star made of two triangles, one with the apex pointing up and the other down. This is a metaphor for 'as above, so below', explaining that all that is in heaven is reflected on Earth. After learning how to be of service in Virgo, as we begin to put this into practice in our lives, we realise that part of our true purpose is to bring heaven to Earth, or rather to be the embodiment of remembering that it is always here.

Libra, the astrological sign at this time, is all about beauty, the mirror, the reflection of what is within. It is the second air sign, another masculine, positive sign. The first, being Gemini, deals with thoughts and the communication between the ego and the higher self. In Gemini we can see the twins at play. In this sign, Libra communicates with the other, the lover, and like Narcissus, falls in love with its reflection. With beauty high on its agenda, theoretical beauty, the beautiful idea becomes very important and so it is symbolised by the scales, the sign of balance, fairness, seeing both sides. It is at this midway point of the year, when the lengths of the days and nights are balanced, that we are truly in a position to begin to make wise judgements. We are idealists, trying to create a perfect world. With all this love and beauty in our hearts, just as we are stepping into the fourth chakra, our heart chakra, we have also arrived at the fourth note of the scale; the perfect fourth as it is called, and its reflection, the perfect fifth, is also the midway point on the scale.[1]

The freedom that this idea of perfection offers is so empowering it is almost terrifying, and we have run away from it, creating gods that do not embody this high ideal. We have belittled the expansive nature of this amazing masculine quality and in doing so have created lesser versions of ourselves. Our gods are judgemental and so are feared, and we have built societies and systems that reflect this. This is the shadow side of the Libra archetype. It is this aspect of our culture that gets involved with warfare, as the idealism loses its way and the Libran generals send the Arian foot soldiers, as willing participants, to fight their battles for them. These are the battles that we are constantly playing out in our hearts projected on to the other.

We can see this on the individual level in many ways, but what fascinates me is how the ego deals with the battleground it has created for itself. As the ego is faced with a chance to grow and embrace ways that were lost but now are being rediscovered, the possibility of healing and finding peace is in sight. The shadow side of our egos, the side that enjoys being in pain and not dealing with the broader issues of life, starts to dig its heels in. This is the shadow aspect of the Narcissus archetype and is now beginning to play its part beautifully. This presence has grown ever stronger in the last few decades with the arrival of technology and our mobile phones. I must admit my ego took a little knock the first time I became aware of this modern manifestation. I was late to come to these phones and was on stage watching a young man take a photo of me. As I tried not to pose I suddenly realised he was not taking a picture of me at all, but was posing for a selfie. I had to refrain from bursting into laughter, as it looked so ridiculous. Now of course it is the norm, with people racking up thousands of photos of themselves as the digital format allows for limitless numbers, it seems. Understanding this desire for multitudes of images of ourselves is a phenomenon that requires investigation. I can see our teenagers needing to come to terms with their new physically grown self-image but this does not serve us to continue into adulthood.

I believe that as we turn our backs on the wisdom of the ages and refuse to let it guide us through our lives then we grow fearful of what lies ahead. Rather than embracing the idea that we shall all die and learn how to accept it we put our heads in the sand and remain spiritual children, clinging on to the physical aspects of ourselves at all costs. It is the outward-looking masculine aspect of ourselves that creates the ability to separate and compartmentalise the world, and when we only allow it to work in the physical dimension it creates in us a feeling of separation from everything around us.

Collecting thousands of images of ourselves in a box sums up this idea of the neediness of the ego and our feelings of separation perfectly. Although I sense this is of course all part of our journey home, I do feel we are taking the longest route, however eventful.

It is widely thought that we have come into this human state of being to experience what it is to be separate from the 'all that is' oneness of the universe. We have to learn what it is to be 'apart' from the oneness to appreciate being 'a part' of it. (I do love the way our English language works.) If you're always hot then you don't appreciate heat. While we are in this state of being human we are also too busy being what we are to appreciate what we truly are. This is more obviously felt when we remember that we're too busy being on this beautiful Earth to realise we're actually travelling at nearly a thousand miles an hour.

So to experience who we are, we use our masculine, creative energy to create a reflection of ourselves in our world around us. We are energy, light, vibration, which is music, we are healing beings and we are love. As we bring all these into our world – using the creative attributes of Libra's opposition, or reflection, Aries – and understand how to live with ourselves through the reflection of the other, we can learn and grow, balance and harmonise. This can be experienced many ways through all our relationships in life. Maybe the most important, which shows us to be the miracle-workers we are, truly bringing heaven to Earth, is through creating a new life as a reproduction of ourselves. As we learn to love our children unconditionally we remember how we are loved. It is this new harmonious state of balance that enables us to raise our vibration and so gain one of the most important keys to the golden city. As I have already stated, this is not a place we shall arrive at but a state of mind we can achieve.

This golden city that we are constantly seeking is that place of peace within; our open hearts. It is important to understand that everything we have in our world around us was created by ourselves, and this is being confirmed by our quantum scientists. As we are created in God's image, so we create our world in our own image. The world appears as it is to us because of our interactions with it, and this creates a sense of personal accountability. This can be a very difficult state of realisation to arrive at, especially when the creative choice is rarely made consciously. When we begin to understand this, the first thing we must learn to do is to remove any feelings of blame. We humans are very good at finding the negative in everything so if there's any fear to be had or finger-pointing to be done we can be very quick to jump to it, especially if we're pointing it at ourselves. The joy is felt when we release the blame and choose to step into a world of taking responsibility for our own actions, knowing we do actually have the power to make the changes we need to enter our hearts. If we have healed the energy in our solar plexus we are on the way to finding that power that has been concealed from us for so long.

It's a wonderful thing to reach that point, knowing that our journey is an attempt to return to oneness of 'all that is'. Yet, it is important to remember that nothing is ever that simple and there are always pitfalls on the way. I began to think that every joyful addition to my life was a positive move towards my golden city and every negative one a move further away. For me, it felt like a game of snakes and ladders and I had to learn not to give myself a hard time if I slipped down to the bottom of the board. As we see that we are given plenty of opportunities to revisit the story in need of healing, we can also realise that even the negative experiences are not actually a step away from the oneness. This can just be our perception; as long as we recognise the experience for what it was, it can all be seen to be forward in motion.

It was at this point in the course, in Libra, that I was introduced to A. T. Mann's map of the twelve astrological months of the year, reflecting the twelve stages of man's lifetime journey. That same day I pulled the book off the shelf that led me to my awareness of the golden city. The title had drawn my attention to it in the first place and I had only read the first page, which was full of pretty heady stuff, but immediately knew I had to read it. So I asked John if I could borrow it. It was self-published and the author, Chrissy Philp, lived nearby. We soon built up a fascinating relationship as she explained her book to me. At first she was amazed at my interest as I was the first person unknown to her who wanted to know about it, and she had written it quite a few years ago. In this book *The Golden City*, she has created a model of the brain, bringing together and reconciling all different belief systems into one grand theory, rather like the unification theory scientists are looking for. She connects the scientific understanding of the brain with astrology, psychology, religion and divination in the form of the I Ching.

Starting with the theory that the brain's two cerebral hemispheres metaphorically carry a masculine and a feminine aspect, the positive and the negative, taking a bird's eye cross-section of the brain she then divides it again with a left-to-right axis. This then gives us the religious Christian cross and the mathematical axes. Taken from Liz Greene's model, placing the four elements, fire, air, earth and water, in the four quarters of the axes, she then places the twelve astrological archetypes, according to their elemental qualities, in harmony with each other, around this circular image. Each psychological aspect and biological attribute of these archetypes relates exactly to the location and cortex of the brain in which they are known to be found. Pairing them horizontally and across the diameters, she explains our life journey from source into being and how we have structured our environment both physically and socially. She then connects them in the order they are found around the year and creates a model, rather like a butterfly, of beautiful and perfect symmetry. She does it again with a model connecting the signs' planetary counterparts in the order they are positioned from the sun and in which they were discovered, and creates another model of perfect symmetry, relating to the DNA strand. These models work according to the old order of astrology, before the outer planets were discovered, equally as well as with the new order. It is an awe-inspiring piece of work and this information is found only in the first half of the trilogy.

At the same time a friend of mine, quite out of the blue, when I turned up at his work one day, handed me a book.

"I was in a second-hand bookshop, saw this and thought of you," he said. "It's a gift."

It was book of mystical arts of the occult, containing chapters on numerology, palmistry, astrology and the I Ching. The I Ching was something I knew nothing about. I felt I needed my own copy and someone to guide me through the workings of it.

As I spent time with Chrissy, I discovered that she lived her life by astrology and the I Ching and she was expert in both. She began teaching me how to use the coin version of the I Ching (you throw three coins six times, like picking a tarot card or a rune, and how the coins fall creates a six-line hexagram which translates into an image and a reading), and as with all my experiences with divination I found it to be both exacting and extremely beautiful. Within a month or two and after some failed attempts at finding my own copy of the I Ching, Andy came home one day with a copy of it in his hand.

"A friend of mine thought you might like this," he said. There it was, an amazing sequence of gifts that started playing itself out even before I knew to ask for it.

I felt my understanding of all these new tools and their place in my view of the universe was deepening. The concept of 'as above, so below', relating so clearly with the Creative Heaven and Receptive Earth hexagrams of the I Ching, was revealing to me that the map of the heavens was being constantly reflected on to the manifest Earth. I began to grasp the idea that our astrological birth chart is a snapshot of the sacred geometry created by the alignments of all the planets at the moment of our birth, offering us a manual to guide us through our lives. As this manual is constantly being updated, we can look at the sky and read its messages at every moment in time, enabling us to see how our birth chart is a starting point from which we can learn and grow. Nothing stays still. As the heavens move, so do we. The I Ching, as I have already said, clearly states this in its title, the translation being *The Book of Changes*.

As I worked my way through Chrissy's book, enjoying every connection she made, making a oneness out of all the subjects we have created into ideas of separation, the idea for my talk was being formed in my mind. With each page I turned she gave more beautiful confirmations of what I was trying to say, and the big moment came for me when I started planning Libra. As I reached the diagram where she divided the brain into the two left and right sides with the masculine, positive astrology signs on one side and the negative, feminine signs on the other, I realised she was showing me the two I Ching hexagrams, the masculine Creative Heaven (six positive or yang lines), the 'all that is' energy, and the feminine Receptive Earth (six negative or yin lines), the manifested third-dimensional world that we inhabit. Here I saw the two I Ching hexagrams created by the twelve astrological archetypes divided into two sections of six. Knowing that all these aspects of our brain

106

are connected, energetically and physically (the brain has twelve pairs of cranial nerves, six on each side), she showed how all the pieces were in place to create any of the sixty-four hexagrams at any moment in time. Her diagrams connecting these twelve points, like spokes in a wheel, showed how they all pass through the central point of the brain, the 'now'. I understood that our brain is a fully functioning divining entity metaphorically throwing the coins every time we are offered a choice or ask a question. The I Ching is purely the manifested reflection of what we already are. The Chinese have created, honed and perfected this over thousands of years.

Once this door had been opened there was obviously no end to it but the another joyous moment for me, as a musician, was in understanding that, when you replace the astrological archetypes with the twelve notes of the chromatic scale, the whole concept of music and how it came about in the scales and form we use today is all just a reflection what we already are. We have created music to reflect how our bodies vibrate and sing and every culture has its own version of its musical cycle. It may be inaudible to us but its power and resonance lie in the very essence of our being. We have forgotten how to listen and manifest our sound, but the birds haven't. They innately sing, unconscious of the fact they are reflecting, answering and manifesting the joy of the energy of the Creative Heaven, the 'all that is' energy.

With this growing correlation between the electro-magnetism of our cells, our own bodies and our auras, and the Earth's magnetic poles giving off its stunning chakra colours in what we call the Aurora Borealis, was a growing awareness of the vibration that is held in all 'bodies.' From the atom to the planets and beyond, everything is creating its own sound, or rather, music. The importance of this was beginning to fully dawn on me.

Within the next few months, two people said to me, "Oh,

I don't have a musical bone in my body." The irony is perfect as that is only their belief of separation from their own internal world of music, and actually every bone in their body is indeed silently singing.

As I pondered on all of this, I remembered that following my regression my question about whether I should have children or not was still very much in the balance for me. I had a healing booked with Louise and during the session she was getting guidance that we would both have children and that they would be twin flames. She asked me to sense a date for the conception of this child. Reluctantly I did, but when I left I must admit I didn't feel comfortable doing this.

I then had a conversation with another friend, Susan, who was also my Reiki teacher and she explained how, when she was young, she had felt that she would gain a greater connection to the 'all that is' energy through love and marriage. When that didn't answer her quest for connection she then hoped she would gain greater connection by having children. Still it wasn't there. Although her experience of motherhood was very enriching for her, she finally came to understand that the connection would only come through her own journey towards her higher understanding of herself.

Through this story and a feeling that motherhood was perhaps not where I was headed, I made the decision not to have children but to try and work more with my healing guides to develop my spiritual connection, hoping that this was my path. With my sun and four other planets in the watery energy of Pisces, decision-making isn't my strong point, particularly when faced with such a huge decision as this, one that you can't go back on.

What helped me make the decision finally was the fact that I knew I was worried that when I got older I might regret my decision. Having realised that I was basing my decision on an unknown future, I decided to make my decision solely on how I felt about it now. Then I had to decide that whatever my decision was I would be happy with it. That was the crunch and as soon as I had stated it, the decision was easy.

A year or so went by and Louise didn't have a child either. She said she didn't feel ready and I totally understood, although I wondered what the guidance was all about.

I began putting my own musical project together and I needed a name for it, and names, in the past, had never come easy to me. I wasn't sure if this would be a stumbling block. It was also at this time that I was given Deepak Chopra's *Synchro-Destiny* to read and I don't know what it was that made me think this but as I picked it up I decided that I would find the name for my new band in this book. As I began to be totally inspired by the whole idea of synchronicity I came across the word *sutura*. This means 'a stitch on the soul', coming from the word 'sutra' meaning mantra and 'suture', a medical stitch. I realised that with this word – the whole concept of the Creative Heaven energy gifted to us through our thought processes being brought into manifestation, the 'Receptive Earth' – I was explaining my whole journey of finding my truth and through my spiritual practice I was able to anchor it into this plane of existence. With my new creative gifts I could now walk my path with love; something I believe we can all do. It was a profound moment for me.

Three years later, in 2007, I had put together a band with my songs on the harp and it was time to record a CD. We began recording at the start of the year but it was proving to be a difficult process. There was nothing I could put my finger on but nothing went smoothly, and although I have recorded many albums in the past, this was the first time I was recording my own music. In that respect I can only put my hand up and say that most of the issues would have been rooted in my lack of confidence and experience in this new role I had taken on. Time ticked on and it wasn't until September that there was an end in sight. Sitting in a café with Susan one day, I remember commenting how this was feeling like a true gestation period. I was creating my first 'baby' in the form of a CD and it had taken nine months to produce. I was also complaining that as the end was approaching I felt as if everyone had run a mile and I was having to complete the final 'birthing' stages all alone. We were having a good laugh at this analogy with some feelings of poignancy when suddenly Susan recalled that our friend Louise, who had given me the guidance about our having twin flames, was about to give birth to her first child that week. I had to admit, I was completely stopped in my tracks. The information had come through four years before and I had dismissed it, as it hadn't seemed to come to pass. Suddenly it reminded me that time is not a factor when it comes to guidance and that one should always be prepared for the broadest of interpretations. We had both fulfilled our fate, bringing into being a piece of our own creation.

As soon as the CD was complete, I visited the new family and gifted them with what I thought was the newborn's twin flame. At the time I truly hoped that they would have a strong bond, as I know I worked hard to manifest a true reflection of myself in this act of creation. I called the album *To Music*. The album title came to me without resistance.

Three years pass, it's 2010 and I have been gifted the book *Zero Limits* by Joe Vitale, which takes all that I have learned about reflection one stage further into the true sense of everything being as one. As I read about a new form of healing, based on the ancient traditional Hawaiian methods, called Ho'oponopono, it reveals how one can heal everything in our world just by working on yourself, an idea I touched upon in Gemini. If we are truly one then our separation is just the illusion and we are all simply a reflection of each other. The author meets a healer who was said to have healed a whole ward of psychiatric patients without even meeting them. He would just utter mantras of love and requests of forgiveness, while pacing the corridors of the hospital, till he had cleansed his energy entirely. He understood that he was responsible for everything within himself and that if he could fully clear out all his closets within, that would automatically reflect on to his external world. It worked to such a degree that they virtually closed the ward; there were no more patients left who needed medical attention. This had a profound effect on me.

At this time, I realised I hadn't written a song for eighteen months as my creativity was heading in other directions and I was beginning to question if I would be able to write another. Had the tap been turned off as suddenly as it had been turned on? Thankfully these questions kick-started me back into action. I began incorporating the mantra I had read in the book into my morning breathing exercises and then I suddenly thought, if I could say them, then surely I could sing them. I went to my harp one day in August 2010 and a song downloaded itself to me in a torrent of words and music.

The words[2] tell a story of a girl looking in the mirror and blaming her reflection for the fact that her life hasn't worked out how she had wanted it to. As the story unfolds and her reflection turns its back on her, we can see that we are, in effect, alone in the room. The words and music came so quickly, with a second song following close behind; it was like they were lining up to come through after the dam had been holding them back for so long.

By the end of the night, I was aware that with all the lyrics I had written down there didn't seem to be an obvious line I could use for a title, so I went to bed with the request for some help there.

That night, my friend, who was also the bass player in my party band until he died suddenly in 2004, came to me in a dream and said, "There's a golden mirror in the sky and it's covered in shit, and we've got to clean it."

"Ooh," I said, "that sounds really difficult."

"Yes it is," he replied, "but we have to do it." There was always a bit of a chuckle in his voice when he communicated with me, and it was certainly there now.

I woke with the words 'golden mirror' in my head. I don't know why I hadn't worked it out for myself; it was such an obvious title in the light of the morning.

When I called Seb to tell her about Rich coming into my dream – they had been very good friends – she was very excited and added, "Yes, it's like the Hubble telescope. If it gets even a speck of dust on it they have to send a whole platoon of astronauts up to clean it."

She was speaking metaphorically of course, and I realised even a speck of dust can distort the image. It was uplifting to know that we have this already happening in reality as we, collectively, have already put this incredible telescope in the sky, a giant mirror, which we are working hard to keep spotless. My desire to clear out my closet, to clean that mirror, gained renewed enthusiasm and I do believe that it was this process that enabled me to bring about the journey which helped me to heal my asthma.

This mirror image stayed with me for quite a while and I began to really enjoy the reflection of it in our lives. One of my favourite lines in my song, *If we don't go within then we go without*, seemed to sum up this idea very cleverly. I can't claim it as my own as it is something I have picked up on my way but I can certainly appreciate the play on words and know we can all learn to live by its teaching.

A little later, I was on the phone to Louise as she had just given birth to her second child. During the conversation she explained to me that she believed that it was this child that was connected to the guidance she had received about the twin flames. Having just birthed my new 'baby' in the form of a talk and healing workshop called *Keys to the Golden City*,

I knew it carried a far more profound vibration than my CD. It seemed we were coming full circle. As the summer progressed and my life took on a challenging process as Andy was moving out and the Grand Cross had come to a pivotal alignment, I put aside the need to investigate this twin flame connection for now.

The New Year brought many new wonderful gifts and I began editing this book. A year had passed since the first draft was written and I realised that this story was still unfinished. Often we can have all the pieces in the bag, but not have the last piece of thread which ties the bag up. I could see how I had brought in so many mechanisms and methods that showed me how I could understand my story; earthly practices that we have created as reflections of the higher workings of our universe. I had also been shown how we carry and embody all this inside ourselves. But I could not see how my life as an individual fit into that mechanism. We all have a yearning to discover our personal role in the story that is being played out on the grand scale.

I picked up the phone to speak to Louise again, a year on from our last conversation. I realised I hadn't tried to pre-empt her answer in my mind as I presumed I would not have a clue what it would be. So when I asked her what she thought her connection with her second child might be that would somehow reflect my connection with my project, I would never have imagined the answer could have been so simple. (I refuse to give myself a hard time at this point even though my inability to engage my brain and remember all that I have learned never ceases to amaze me. Of course, I knew the answer was going to be simple. Who was it that said, *The answer to life, the universe and everything had to be simple. If it were complicated, we'd all get it?* I do love that.) Louise replied to my question by saying that her daughter was a Christ child, in fact both of them were, as the two children were the twin flames, one of which I could have conceived, should I have wished to take that path. She said the guidance was saying that I should not feel any guilt about my choice and I assured her I didn't.

What I was feeling was that one door was closing and another beautiful new journey was just beginning. As my dream of this utopian world was becoming a reality inside myself I could feel the illusion that I could see before me, that we call reality, begin to crumble before my eyes. The desire to pull all the resources that we are shown, reflected in the first half of our progression through the seasons, was rising through me, filling my heart with an understanding of how to move forward through life in a profound and positive way. I had chosen not to marry or to have children and was putting all my energy into creating the marriage within. How this would play out as my life progressed from here I would have to wait and see. I was discovering the immense power of the heart, physically, electromagnetically and emotionally, and my desire to deepen my connection with the Christ consciousness was growing daily. It felt like an immense and profound sigh slowly releasing itself within me and expanding my whole sense of being. It was a clear and perfect reflection.

Chapter 8

Behind the Looking Glass

Sebastian

She came like an eagle in the springtime of my life,
Swooping through my open door like a mountain in flight.
Promising gifts of gold and riches of your dreams,
But you were circling way above our heads, Sebastian.

Like a bee to a flower I sought the colours of your life.
Guiding each other through troubled days and troubled nights.
But like shadows in the darkness you kept yours hidden well.
You were the fortress on the hill and only I heard the warning bell.

And the storm raged deeper and wilder than I could have dreamed.
And the thunder ripped you apart at the seams.
And the lightning struck a chord of vision in your heart.
And I saw you as if for the first time, Sebastian.

She came like an angel on the stillness of the breeze
Lifting my heart to show the gold buried there.
The riches of my dreams are the hopes I can fulfil

And though you show me the way you cannot stay, Sebastian.

And the storm raged deeper and wilder than I could have dreamed.
And the thunder ripped you apart at the seams.
And the lightning struck a chord of vision in your heart.
And I saw you as if for the first time, Sebastian.

The leaves have fallen. They are now lying on the ground, rotting, forming the compost that gives life and nutrients for next year's spring growth; the phoenix that will rise from the ashes. We are now arriving at the last stage of adulthood, from forty-two till death, and are not just learning to die; we are now preparing to die. I believe we are shown this seasonal cycle every year of our lives, seeing the death and rebirth of Mother Nature, in the hope that we will understand that we are seeing our own life in miniature. This is the Russian doll symbol in the form of time; cycles within cycles, the year reflecting our whole life journey. Every year we await the arrival of spring and breathe a sigh of relief when it comes, as if it could be in doubt. Yet in the same way, we doubt our own rebirth. This doubt comes from fear and it's the fear that becomes our greatest enemy, for in fearing death we also fear life, and what we fear most in life is what lies in the murky, watery depths of our inner psyche.

It is at this time that we celebrate Halloween, or Samhain as it was originally called by our ancestors. It is believed that this is the time of year when the veil is thin. As Mother Earth begins her journey towards death, the separation between the physical and the spirit worlds almost feels like it has evaporated, the veil has dropped and we can easily communicate with those who have passed over if we choose to. This communication is different, working through the emotions and our psychic abilities. For some this seems terrifying and out of our fears and loss of understanding, we have removed all the beauty and solemnity from this important point on our journey. This is our chance to honour those who have come before us and reconnect in a way that can empower us and broaden our view of the world we inhabit. Instead, we have introduced rituals which have reduced it to a commercial event of just dressing up and sweets. We have also created a whole genre of horror films designed to cut ourselves off from our emotions and deal with fear in a way that surely doesn't serve us.

We are now in the astrological month of Scorpio. Another water sign, the yin, the feminine, the receptive essence of ourselves, and this sign invites us to investigate our shadow as it is ruled by Pluto, or Hades, god of the underworld. It deals with the issues we are most afraid to look at, which have become taboo in today's society, subjects such as sex and death. This is probably the deepest and most transformational of signs and enables us, if we are brave enough, to get in touch with our sixth sense.

If we learn to trust, to get to grips with our fear, we can dare to open the door or lift the lid on what we have kept firmly shut for so long. As we choose to peek behind the veil, into that world beyond the physical, what we initially discover is that the issue is never as bad as we thought. What we had kept hidden for all this time, the monster, the dragon that needed slaying, was seeded in our imagination that is caught up in fear. We also discover that it is purely our shadow side, a vital part of who we are. This is what makes us whole, the Taoist yin to match the yang. When we lift the lid and let the light shine in on this dark abyss, we balance ourselves again and gain another key to the golden city, raising our vibrations still higher.

Jesus understood this and said that what you bring forth from within you will save you. What you keep hidden within will destroy you.[1]

This transformational journey that we may take in Scorpio

enables us to step into the higher chakras. These are the reflection of the lower three chakras; the Creative Heaven energy of 'all that is' mirroring the Receptive, Manifest Earth. However, it seems that not everybody needs to make this shift to look at what lies beyond. The journey into these higher chakras is not always necessary because the heart chakra, acting as the bridge between the two, being another reflection of 'all that is', contains all the other chakra energies within it and many are quite content to remain there. It is rather like the white light that, as it enters the prism, reveals all the seven colours of the rainbow spectrum within it.

There is also another way, as some choose to take a different route to the other side. There are many people who, at this seemingly early time of life, pass over, experiencing the ultimate human transformation. Elvis was one, and Hollywood actress Natalie Wood drowned at the age of forty-three, which I heard was something she greatly feared. My paternal grandfather was another. Others have near-death experiences to nudge them into taking a more in-depth view of their lives once they've returned, after having had a serious peek beyond the veil. For most us this time, which is often called the mid-life crisis, is just an invitation to develop a deeper outlook on life. I was only just realising the significance of this as I was experiencing this transformational stage in my life at forty-two.

Having recently read Eckhart Tolle's *A New Earth*, which I highly recommend if you haven't already, he put all that I had been thinking about neatly into a few words. He explains how the whole aspect of youth is concentrated on outward, physical growth, the expansion of form. As we reach adulthood and maturity, the physical body begins to degenerate, like the leaves on the trees in autumn, and our thoughts should then turn from outward, physical form towards the inner, spiritual aspects of life. Our society has completely shut the door on this part of our journey. We have become afraid of anything beyond death and have closed our eyes to anything beyond our physical existence. This leaves us living in fear of this transition and are now doing everything in our power to prevent reaching it at all. We have created a society of adults who do not wish to grow up spiritually and so the youth culture has become king.

When we decide, culturally, that we can face our fear we will begin to understand that this world in which we live is just an illusion. Wearing our human suit, we are just a reflection of the cosmic 'all that is' energy, learning how to appreciate being separate from it so we can return with joy to our true spirit selves. Then we may learn that death is just a door we all open and step through, and that peeking behind the curtain whilst we are here is not some form of madness or to be rubbished, but an exciting glimpse of what exists all around us and indeed within us.

With this discovery and all the work I had done with my father, I knew I needed to investigate my journey with my mother, which would balance this. My mother has her sun in Scorpio and my Neptune is in Scorpio. Neptune is all about the unseen, what lies behind the veil, and so is Scorpio. My relationship with my mother, as I first began to view it, seemed not to reflect this in any way. Our relationship is wonderful, she is an intellectually deep, interesting woman with many talents and we can discuss anything for hours, personal or worldly. However, she is her mother's daughter and for years she had been unable to escape my grandmother's influence. I never knew my great-grandparents but I suppose the line must continue back. My grandmother, whose inheritance I gained with my house, was also a highly intelligent, worldly woman. She left school at twelve when the First World War began and became a self-made businesswoman. Although she missed out on an education you would never have known as she was so well-read. I'm sure she must have given up a good deal to make a life for herself and her family, as so many immigrants did at that time, and this is what may have made her so hard on herself and those close to her. As a direct recipient of her gifts I now understand that I must honour all that hard work and all that she denied herself so that I can enjoy the fruits of her labour.

She was a well-loved woman, however, if you were a direct descendant of hers the road was a little more complex. Never wanting to be knowingly unkind, she had subtle ways of showing her powerful negativity. In the past year I have worked hard on this negative view I have of my grandmother and with the passing of time, my mother only remembers her with fondness and I am now learning to do the same. Knowing that in death she is now approving of my work, I have had to offer a huge belated thank-you to her for the gift of my beautiful house and all her wealth of mental and physical abundance she brought into this world. The negativity is mine and mine alone; she let go of it when she passed on and probably never saw herself in this way anyway. That was just my image of her.

However, my mother did grow up in this environment, and coupled with the fact that she was six when the Second World War broke out, her whole faith in humanity was crushed. She would often tell me of her fears of her own death she held as a child. She does agree that as she has got older this has calmed down but up until a year or so ago, I felt that she was in denial of any connection to her sun sign. Whereas my father was, at first, fearful of my journey, as he was quite close to opening his door, even if it was just a crack, it seemed my mother was choosing to ignore the door to such an extent that she was not even aware of it. I was under the impression she didn't accept there was anything beyond the physical world.

My father's positive influence encouraged my mother to

transform herself from a mother and housewife, although that in itself is never to be underestimated, to a woman willing to explore her many creative strengths.

When asking my father if she was capable of doing an A Level, not long after having me, rather than trying to boost her ego, he just replied, "Anyone can do an A Level." My father had such an easy way about him you couldn't help but feel positive about yourself.

My mother went on to do three A Levels, a degree, open a shop, write a book, a play, some short stories – the list will not stop until she becomes physically and mentally unable to do anything. We are all so proud of her, however, I was continually aware of a lack of confidence and a feeling that she didn't sit comfortably with her achievements. I saw this mirrored in myself too. We would tell each other off for our own negativity about ourselves, but I know mine came from her and hers came from her mother and so on. I feel now I have found my real vocation, my self-doubt has been reduced to a very small voice that I hardly hear anymore. I have only recently come to realise that this is being mirrored in my mother too.

My mother allowed me to discuss all the ins and outs of my new discoveries with her and I am very grateful to her for that, and for a while I believed that none of it touched her, but as the years have passed and as I have healed more and more aspects of myself, I have become aware of subtle changes in the way she relates to my work. It is with great joy that I have found her agreeing with me in discussions whereas years before I would have had to stand alone in my beliefs. Most importantly, she has stated a real sense of having healed many aspects of her past and her relationship with her mother and can look back at her journey without pain. With this knowledge, I had arrived at a place where I truly believed I had healed my asthma. But unbeknown to me, something was rising up from behind the veil, dark and unseen. For the moment, however, it would stay hidden in the shadows and I remained oblivious to it, aware only of what I could see in the light.

As I am able to view both my parents with so much respect and love, I know this has brought balance into my life, obtaining this very important key to the golden city. I feel this has enabled me to have a positive outlook on even the seemingly negative things in life, like death, however odd that might sound. I have been lucky enough in my life so far not have lost too many loved ones. My first real experience of loss was a very wonderful uncle who died when I was in my early twenties. I have to say my lack of experience was obvious, as I could not even utter his name in the presence of my aunt for fear of what it might trigger for her, even many years after his passing. My grandmother died a few years later, but it wasn't until the millennium year that I had to start dealing with it in a big way. Although no one really close to me died, it seemed like people around me were dying, young and old, every month or so. This was all part of that first, very transformational year for me as I began to learn all about healing, and though at the time I called it 'the year of death' I suppose I should have entitled it 'the year of transformation'.

Four years later in 2004 and there it was. Our close friend, Rich, the bass player in my party band, following a minor bike accident had two blood clots and died almost instantly. It was the most shocking thing I had experienced, as it was so sudden and he was so young. Our lives went into turmoil and our house became a centre for people to connect and grieve his loss. My main energy was soon being focused on his girlfriend who was seeking refuge with Andy and I, as friends who were amongst those closest to him. I had just recently taken my Reiki 1 course and it seemed fitting to offer it. As a doctor of science, I was not sure she would be interested but I think at that point she was clutching at straws and was just hoping to find anything that could help. I had never been so close to a friend suffering so much trauma, and I could only hope that I could be of some help. She was my gift and I hoped that I was hers. If I doubted my abilities as a Reiki practitioner, she was able to offer me the chance to experience just how powerful it can be. The lesson was that, of course, Reiki has a wisdom and power that goes beyond the facilitator. We are just the channel, and even doubt won't prevent it working as long as the receiver is open to it. Knowing that it was my friend who got her life back on track, she understood that the work we did helped her to reach that place in a way that she could heal her wounds by getting in touch with her inner strength and finding her truth. She constantly amazed me.

For months following the main body of sessions we did, she would often return saying, "Vicki, I need rebalancing." It was so wonderful for me to hear a scientist crossing that illusionary divide into the world of healing.

After this difficult episode facing trauma head on, I realised I had always feared other people's emotions far more than my own. In my song *Sebastian*, that I wrote as a thank-you for my friend in 2002, I try to convey just how she had to rip herself apart, lifting the lid on what she had been hiding from herself, so that she could plunge into the depths of her inner world. Only then could she transform and rise like the phoenix. She took that fearful path and certainly came out shining on the other side. Recognising the joy that comes from what may seem like a very painful experience, we are now ready to embrace whatever life may bring.

The following year I was exposed to a life-changing experience on the eve of buying my harp, during which I was gifted my own taste of the other side. This was most incredible moment of my life, beyond words (though I will give it a go in Chapter 12), and as I talked about it to others,

I sensed it was like a little taster of a near-death experience, without the trauma of nearly dying. Following this, I found it difficult to feel sorrow for myself or my departed friend. I felt joy, knowing that he was enjoying a state of true bliss and only felt grief for those enduring his loss.With this whole journey came an understanding that I had a role to play to help people through this process. I started by making sure that I always phoned people when they had lost a loved one. Although cards are very important because they become keepsakes, I think as so many people are scared to speak to people during the grieving process, it's very important that they have a chance to talk, let their emotions out and speak openly about the person they have loved and lost. We, in our modern society, have hidden these processes behind closed doors, forgetting that it's the ritual that helps us through it. It's the community that should wrap you up and hold you through these painful times. However, I feel we have cut ourselves off from each other into our little separate lives, where the ego, the physical form and the mistaken importance of the individual are held supreme. This then leads to loneliness and an inability to grieve properly when a loved one dies.

As our dark night of the soul reaches its climax and we, as a society, grow increasingly disconnected from each other and our spiritual world, our fear of death seems to become ever more heightened. The other day I was very saddened to hear of a middle-aged woman who in her will decreed that there should be no funeral for her. She left two teenage children who were denied the chance of processing her leaving and I can only hope they find the wisdom to work it through themselves. A close friend of mine told me that when she missed her grandmother's funeral, because she didn't have the money to travel to the country where it was being held, she didn't sleep for six months. At the time she didn't understand the reason for her sleeplessness until her sister offered her this connection. She never missed another funeral after that, however far the distance.

Ritual is an ancient gift passed down to us through the millennia. The importance of rituals has been understood for so long and only now are we believing that we know better, even though we are aware that fear is our only guide. Again, no judgement, only sadness for those who are being denied this ancient wisdom.

Four years after my friend has died, it's 2008, and as I arrived at our day of Scorpio on John's astrological course he was playing music that we were invited to dance to. Within minutes I got it. I had a eureka moment and almost felt I'd completed the day's work then and there. I realised that, as my life was so blessed and filled with light, I had thought I didn't really have a shadow side, or not one worth investigating anyway. How wrong I was; how naïve! We all have fears and a dark side that needs recognising and inviting in from the cold. I knew then and there that I was going to have to change this view of my life and take a deeper, darker road for a while. Being blessed with this amazing Alchemical Journey enabled me to recognise the fear I was facing at that moment, as I was already in the process, irrespective of my feelings of denial, of splitting from my long-term partner.

Later in the day John set up an exercise, where we each donned a gold cloak and then covered it with a black cape. We had to sit in the centre and declare to the rest of the group our deepest fears and then we could remove the black cape to reveal the gold beneath. I didn't feel I really engaged with the exercise on the day. It was a huge door for me and I would need to approach it in my own time. When I did actually face all those fears, the image of that golden cloak kept me going through it.

At the end of that very powerful and explorative day the breadth of the archetypal gifts were still becoming apparent.

John went through our charts and looking at mine, he said, "You should be working with the dying," because I had my sun in the eighth house and the eighth house is Scorpio, of course.

"I am," I replied.

I had for many years, and still do, play my harp at the local cancer charity, Penny Brohn Cancer Care, as I described in Chapter 1. It was wonderful to feel that I was fulfilling my true path as set out in my chart. However, dealing with my empathy and feeling the pain held by others is something I carry heavily. I knew that working with the dying can be very challenging and I honour those who carry out this work daily. For me it is still very occasional. Helping me to handle this pain with a light heart was the understanding that death is just a part of life; we are all dying, just some are getting there faster than others.

Suffering is such an important part of life that enables us to grow, learn empathy and journey into our shadow side, yet it is again something our society runs away from. We wrap ourselves in cotton wool so we shouldn't feel any pain and so deny ourselves many aspects of life, even the good ones, just in case something goes wrong. But I feel the quote that Jesus offers at the beginning of this chapter says it all, and without suffering you cannot fully understand joy. Balance is essential. At the beginning of the day, John had offered us a quote that said if you ignore your shadow side you become a cardboard angel. That struck a chord, and it was not striking in a good way. Did I have the capability of becoming a fully-fledged angel graduating from even the second to the third dimension?

I had acknowledged I could help others through their fears but was still not fully facing my own. Knowing I had now reached this Scorpionic stage of my life, I had spent this year dealing with the initial stages of the breakdown of my relationship with Andy. As we cried most days, I sensed I was reaching a part of me I had not journeyed to before. Until this moment I think I still believed there was a glimmer of hope of making it work, however, that was just the illusion we were clinging to in our pain. Recognising that I had reached a new vantage point held many mixed emotions. They were mostly ones of deep sadness and fear of what life could hold beyond the relationship. As I could begin to see that we were probably not going to make it, there grew a balancing sensation of elation thrown into the pot. This was not an emotion of the ego; this was my soul showing me I was growing. I was sensing that I was learning to work through my pain so I could come through the other side shining. When we are blessed with experiences like these in our lives it is most definitely time to take stock and truly honour these moments. For me it's a gratitude that knows no bounds.

So how was I to gain this very important key to the golden city, after all that had been gifted to me so far? If I was hoping to move forward from this, I now had to discover whether I had it in me to fulfil all that was being asked.

By the time I reached the summer of 2009, the ThetaHealing course I attended gave me the opportunity to witness some very profound breakthroughs in the lives of some of those on the course with me. At the time, my reason for going on the course was to try another healing tool for healing my asthma. However, by the time I was on the second day, I realised there must be more to it than that. Did I really think I had come just to try another technique? My friend Chrissy used to say, "Never say 'try', just do it." Was I on the course, perhaps, to learn a new healing method to help others? I knew all this was true, but I knew there was something far more profound underlying it all. During the course we were asked to read people's bodies psychically, visualise their angels and learn many exercises to clear held beliefs within our bodies on all levels. These I did with mixed measures of confidence although I was never found lacking more or less than anyone else. On the last day, for one exercise, we were asked to pair up and then find and remove beliefs we were holding as fears. What were my fears? I couldn't think. My partner for this exercise was experiencing the same dilemma. Then it came to me. What I fear most is not fulfilling my highest potential, being what I'd always seen myself as – a 'B' student rather than an 'A' student. That was me in school and all through life; I had always been 'good' but never excelled. I told my partner that I wanted to remove this fear of not being the best I could be and she completely agreed, saying she felt the same about herself.

I met some wonderful people on that course but got to know one woman in particular during that short time, called Cathy. The last exercise we did as a group was to give each other a psychic reading whilst blindfolded and it just so happened that Cathy was my partner for this. It was a very simple reading and I could tell she felt embarrassed at how little she had to offer because she tried to add to it afterwards, as if the initial reading wasn't enough. She said she saw a field with two horses in it, one black and one white, and that they were not really doing anything. I said I thought that was lovely as I lived in a very small village with horses in many of the surrounding fields, so maybe she was seeing my home? After we'd all departed she then sent me a text with information about white stallions and their shamanic symbolism and was excited because she had remembered I'd said I was a Fire Horse in Chinese astrology.

The following day I had booked myself on a sound healing course; this was the summer holidays and I was filling it with lots of wonderful healing events. The course was held in Glastonbury and I had only got home the night before from the ThetaHealing course in Wales. So, in my usual manner, I was slightly disorganised in finding the centre and was late. I went straight into the first session without being able to take stock of my surroundings. At the first break we all went out to the back of the house, which had a beautiful view of the Tor, and there it was: Cathy's reading. I saw two horses in a field not really doing much. One was black and the other white, and minimal fencing separated them from each other because, as someone later explained to me, you can't put stallions together. I was bursting to tell someone and although I didn't know anyone on this course, I knew it would be a great icebreaker and I couldn't and didn't keep it to myself.

At the end of the session, I immediately sent a text to Cathy and told her I'd found her two horses and she was delighted. A few days later she was returning to Bristol from work in Devon and so we arranged for her to pass through my village en route. We had a great catch-up and I was so pleased to hear she was continuing to delve into her amazing psychic abilities as she had some great stories for me. As I told her about the field, she then asked if it was sloping.

I said, "Yes, it was sloping down to the river."

"There was a river!" she burst out.

Now she knew her reading was truly correct, as she had seen exactly my view from the house in Glastonbury. We were both very excited. She then proceeded to pull out a book from her bag.

"I was guided to give you this," she said.

It was Paulo Coelho's *The Valkyries* that I mentioned in Chapter 2. My first reaction, because I was not good at receiving or allowing my abundance to flow, was to say, "Thanks so much but I've already read it, is there someone else who might like it?"

I knew as soon as I had said it how ungrateful that sounded and I began back-pedalling fast. We all know that if you read a book one year you could read a whole new set of understandings into it the following year. I also knew that I had an extremely connected woman in my midst and if she said she was guided to give this book to me, I should accept it graciously. And so I did.

Realising it had been about seven years since I'd read this book, I rediscovered that the author sets out to find his angel; he wants to see it with his own eyes. To reach this goal he has to go through a whole process in the desert and one thing he has to do is break a pact. The leader of the Valkyries tells him we all come into this world making a pact with ourselves that we will not fulfil our true potential. Therefore, in order to step beyond this realm of the ordinary, so can we find the extraordinary within, we have to break this pact with ourselves. The synchronicity could not have been more perfect – well, it always is, isn't it? – and I knew this was what I was going to have to do. The next day I prepared a large circle of my most powerful crystals and put myself through an extensive Theta Healing process.

The following year, when I had been presenting my performance for some time and was thinking about putting my introductory chakra workshop together, I was doing some DIY when it came to me. I was given an image showing that we, as a culture, are all stuck in our root chakra. When this chakra is closed it carries energy that holds on to fear. This revelation brought the understanding that for five hundred years we have been journeying through a dark night of the soul, travelling further away from spirit. Knowing that we are immersed in a society that clings to fear, the tears started to roll down my face. I felt it was being communicated to me that I had to help people step out of this atrophy so they could raise their vibration and step into their heart energy once more. Here I was again, being offered more signposts on my journey back to the golden city, and as I opened myself to understanding the work that needed to be done, the gifts simply started pouring in.

It is this idea of our mortality, or even our immortality, personified by the wounded healer, Chiron, that rules Virgo, that offers us the necessary healing. Accepting and understanding this knowledge that we are going to physically die can free us from our fear of death and enables us to step fully into our experience of life. The links between Virgo and Scorpio are clearly etched into the Greek wisdom with the story of Persephone the virgin being dragged into the underworld by its god, Pluto. This mirrors our journey through the months of the year and our chakras helping us to find our way through our own life story.

There was a growing sense that a huge obstacle had been dealt with and fear was becoming an ever-diminishing issue for me. When I spoke to people about the projects I have embarked on, many of them said how brave or courageous I'd been. I did feel I was at last coming from the heart ('courage' coming from the French word *coeur*, meaning heart), but I didn't feel like courage, as we understand it, was something I was working with. We can all recognise that when we finally discover our divine purpose and begin to walk that path that there is no sense of bravery needed here. There is just that knowing that there is a destination to reach and a deep sense of gratitude that now everything is in flow. There is simply a feeling of great relief as everything seems to come easily, and that we are at last capable of fulfilling all aspects of our lives. The more I trusted, the more the fear just dissolved before me.

Chapter 9

The Quest for a New Voice

Take One

Take one life, offer the stars.
Choose a world from Venus to Mars.

Break down the walls, don't close a door in their face.
The universe calls, connect them to the whole human race.
Nothing's more frightening than the great unknown.
With thunder and lightning, show them all that can be shown.

Take a sip from the flower of life,
Let it slip from one mouth to another.
With one kiss, let love fill our world.

Break down the walls, don't close a door in my face.
The universe calls, connect me to the whole human race.
Nothing's more frightening than the great unknown.
With thunder and lightning, show me all that can be shown.

Take your time, there are so many moments.

Choose your line, your future is your past.
Remember you can learn by design.

Break down the walls, don't close a door in my face.
The universe calls, connect me to the whole human race.
Nothing's more frightening than the great unknown.
With thunder and lightning, show me all that can be shown.

Take one life, what wonder will be when you
Break down the walls, don't close a door in my face.
The universe calls, connect me to the whole human race.
Nothing's more frightening than the great unknown.
With thunder and lightning, show me all that can be shown.
Take me home.

It's winter. Mother Nature seems to have died. On the surface the big breathing out of growth has ceased and she is now taking her big breath in. As we now know, death is not an end, it's a transformation. The seed has simply gone underground and is being germinated in Mother Earth's belly. In our lifetime journey we have now stepped over to the other side. We have died, returning to source to be reborn in our own mother's belly. As we are now cosmic beings and no longer tied to third-dimensional laws of time and location, we are in the quantum state of being both spirit beings and in the foetal stages of life. In his book *The Divine Life*, A. T. Mann shows how this first stage in the womb is fundamental in forming who we are, or rather who we will become. He relates how our mother's awareness at this early stage of her pregnancy, and her realisation of her ability to create, reflects our own creativity in life.

As we see these months every year of our life, if we have chosen to take the transformational journey offered to us by the Pluto archetype and wandered into the underworld, we have now seen the light; we are on a mission from God, but it's our light and our god.

Returning to the last of the fire signs, Sagittarius is symbolised by the archer. Chiron, the wounded healer, was a centaur who traded his life with Prometheus. Wounded beyond repair and unable to die because he was immortal, this exchange of lives with a mortal enabled him to die and transcend to a higher dimension. In this transaction he also gifted humans with the knowledge of fire. We can see the beautiful process through the fire signs as we started by creating the fire in Aries, tended the fire in Leo, and here we are aiming our bow and fiery arrow to spread it far and wide in Sagittarius.

We are now ready to step into the throat chakra, the fifth chakra and the fifth note in the major scale. This is the first of the higher chakras, which are a reflection of the three lower chakras. This fifth chakra is all about truth and communication of a deeper nature, so it is from here that we begin to speak our new truth and spread the news with our archery skills. We are like the newborn, very excitable, very exuberant; like the child who is learning to speak for the first time.

The West carries this archetypal energy and America, like the figurehead, carrying the banner of the West's ideals, is considered the true Sagittarian; it has been associated with the evangelist, the born-again. As America is such a young country you can see their youthful exuberance in all their ideas, wanting everyone to believe them too. The search for truth is written at the top of the banner and this has brought the world into the modern age we have now, but of course, it has its shadow side. You can see the ancient world bristle as this new way, that began in Europe, of imperialism, capitalism and now consumerism, is forced on them. It is because of this relationship that we have the growth of fundamentalism in our world today. As our quest for answers gathers momentum, whether it is for scientific, spiritual or economic truth, extreme views have begun to find their voice. Fundamentalism can now be found in all walks of life and especially in many religions.

The search for truth. This is man's lifelong quest, as a race and as individuals, and for me it will not end until the day I die. I do believe the only way to find your truth is by discovering yourself first. When you find your truth you also need to find your voice. As I believe every living cell is a reflection of the universe and the universe is a reflection of every cell, once we have found our own answers then this will reflect our truth about the whole.

Some scientists have looked into this idea in their research into holograms. It has been found that if you take a section of a hologram it will not show just the part of the image. For example, if you took a hologram of a man and then took the section of his foot, if viewed separately it would still just show a hologram of the whole man again. Each part contains the whole within it. I'm always very excited when the scientific findings match the ancient understandings of the world, even though they are not always believed to be the truth by all. With science it's usually just a case of time. Some scientists have had to wait decades for their theories to be recognised while the rest of the world sits in a state of thinking it knows a truth when it actually is being taught to believe something soon to be proved wrong. The more we can begin to accept that we do not have all the answers, the more we can grow. I also believe this will come in time, but as we know, time doesn't exist, or not as we see it anyway.

When I began learning all about my new vision of the universe, I related my gathering of knowledge to a shopping trip. Each new piece of knowledge I gained was like buying something off a shelf. At the start I could only handle buying things off the bottom shelf, the 'easy to comprehend' ideas, like learning about chakras and auras and energy. However,

I knew there were ideas on shelves higher up that stretched into infinity that I just wasn't ready to buy yet. As the years passed and my ability to grasp broader ideas grew, I bought more and more information off higher and higher shelves. I began to realise that this was a natural progression and that I would eventually be able to handle buying all the ideas, just as I was also buying the idea that linear time does not exist.

Time is not linear as we perceive it, but concurrent like tracks on a CD. All timelines, past, present and future, exist at the same time but we are just choosing this track to play right now. So if time does not run in a linear way, then I have already bought every idea off every shelf, so I might as well save time and take all the ideas home with me now. I needed to stop doubting and be more open to every concept, however 'out there' it sounded. (I also had to trust myself to discern between information that came to me as truth and information that came with an agenda attached. I listened to my inner feelings and guidance to keep me on the right track.) I then began to see that being open to something was very different to knowing it to be true; that would need personal experience. Once I was open to an idea, I would then wait for my own experience, taking comfort in the fact that it would come sooner rather than later. I proved myself right every time with the smaller issues. For the bigger ones, I'll have to wait.

I was also interested to see how each individual's truth can change and grow as their wisdom increases. One of my favourite books when I was younger was Robert Pirsig's *Zen and the Art of Motorcycle Maintenance*, another book about a search for truth. He says how no one shouts about known truths, only ideas that are in question like politics or religion. He states that no one is going to become fanatical about whether the sun is going to rise tomorrow.[1]

This concept resonated with me at the time but now, twenty years later, my perception of the world has grown slightly broader and now I realise that the sun does not rise every morning at all. In fact the sun stays relatively still and we turn, so that the sun appears to rise, and in that sense the sun rises at different times for all of us depending on where we are on the planet. We all have our own version of the truth. So what seemed like solid, immovable truths twenty years ago can now feel like the shifting sands.

Finding my truth is one thing, expressing it to others is quite another. I understood that many people, hearing my beliefs and those of people who live by the same ideals, would call me 'New Age'. Yet these views can be found among the most ancient beliefs of the world and I received this beautiful confirmation when I read a book called *The Hermetica*, which dates back five thousand years just in the written form. I was overjoyed.

It's a wonderful thing, when we are searching for answers, to feel the past coming up to help us forward. My awakening, that life-changing evening at Seb's flat at the age of thirty-two, showed me I had been searching for something, even though I didn't really know I was looking. My Jewish upbringing didn't open any doors for me and as a teenager I dabbled with a few spiritual groups without realising why. When I was fourteen I joined my local Baptist youth group because all my friends seemed to be becoming active Christians and I was just interested in what it was all about. By the time I was seventeen I was ready to close the door on that stage of my life. It made me realise I was a firm atheist and very cynical.

I recalled my last conversation with the Baptists as I was preparing to say goodbye. I remember asking them, "So why do you believe we're here, then?" I must have sounded very sure of myself and quite derisive.

One of my friends explained that they believed that when we die we will form one soul which will be the bride for God, and that there is going to be a great marriage in heaven. At the time I had to stop myself from laughing out loud; the concept sounded quite ridiculous. However, I was young and it would be some years before I would learn about Bruno Bettelheim's understanding of marriage as the marriage within, and realise I would have to start opening my mind a little. It would take another decade or so before I would hear the concept that humanity is about to experience an awakening on a grand scale. I felt humbled in my recollection of this event, realising that I was hearing someone's story, their way of understanding a truth that I was ignorant of and judging them for it. Knowing that my knowledge of the marriage we are all going to experience is just another way of telling the same story brought me back down to earth.

At twenty, I found my horizons broadened exponentially when I travelled to Hong Kong with a pop band I had joined. During this trip we met an amazing woman who taught us a little about Eastern spirituality and how to meditate. However, it wasn't long before events drew me away from continuing my experiments with this new spiritual practice. Although I stood firm in my atheistic beliefs, in the years that followed, I felt a key had been turned for me. The key would spend many years on a shelf before it would be needed again.

As I looked back, I remembered some of the concepts the woman in Hong Kong had taught me. She explained that she viewed the Earth's core as our god and taught me a meditation where we concentrated on breathing light from this core energy in the same way as trees absorb nutrients through their roots. Now this seems absolutely normal, but back in 1986, I'd never heard of this before. She also offered interesting insights into the idea of Venus holding the energy of the fifth dimension and how we were soon to be stepping into that planetary energy ourselves. Again, although I was a little older and I could hear her ideas I wasn't sure how or where to place them in my realm of understanding.

Recognising that I was finding it difficult to take these new concepts on board I stored them, like I have stored all things I haven't felt comfortable with at the time and waited till the moment was right to dust them off and take them down from the high shelf. These nuggets of truth given to me by various different people from various different cultures and parts of the world were all just jigsaw pieces I was picking up on the way to learn how to find my own truth.

With this emerging awareness I was, at the same time, realising that the best way to find one's truth was by listening to yourself, by finding your own voice. After gathering so many different points of view, so often I would receive guidance from very wonderful healers only to discover that, however well intentioned they were, the information that came through was always coloured by their own voice. The clearest voice to listen to had to be your own.

But what have we done with our voice? It has taken us millennia to close our world down to the point where we have forgotten we have a voice. Ancient wisdom, that our indigenous people around the world still live by, was built into our hard drives, in our DNA, and used to inform us in every walk of life. As we have switched this inner voice off through the ages, we have given a voice to new ideas that have only been around a few centuries. These new ways of working, built on a purely physical understanding of the world, tell us our ancient ways are out of date and useless. In losing our voice we have given our power away and empowered those who do not have our best interests at heart because they too have lost touch with their inner guidance. The new truths we are told to believe are based on knowledge and not wisdom, and some of it is not standing the test of time. Although we have lost our own inner voice it still speaks to us, but sadly, we have forgotten how to listen.

For those who still can connect to their inner voice, it is

important to use it to guide our external voice, however that might manifest itself. If we think of our voice as our truth, our own way of being put into the world, then there are as many different voices as people and this should be celebrated. When we learn to trust this we can stop putting our faith in those who have no interest in us as unique individuals. With new developments supposedly designed to work for the good of all, we can begin to see how they really only benefit the world of finance rather than people. This is our time to start believing in ourselves once more and stop fearing what would happen if we stood up and spoke our truth.

At the age of thirty-three, after having my first revelation, within a year I had found a healer who would offer me the most important healing of my life, which gave me a new voice; I just didn't realise it at the time. This expanding world I was stepping into was so rich with inspirations, epiphanies and miracles, I was, although still very excitable, almost getting blasé. At this one session, Louise, my healer, told me that I had a creative block and asked if I would like it removed. Well, what a question – of course I did. Although I was a competent saxophonist, though as I have said, not an entirely satisfied one, I had also written about five songs in twenty years but thrown four of them away. Whenever I had tried to write before I had always been too concerned with being completely original and wanting to be clever. It was like trying to get blood from a stone. Lots of trying involved and lots of head stuff, no allowing or just being.

Louise waved her magic wand and said the appropriate words and within a week I had the first download of a song in the form of a dream. Whenever I get in touch with my guides there is always a good deal of humour involved, as they re-mind me how overly serious I can be, and I woke up laughing. This dream involved the party band I had been in for many years, which only played cover versions. The song, although completely generic, was new to me, so clearly an original. Having a wonderful sentiment, it was called *Living the Days of Love* (complete with a little shimmy dance which I decided to drop, sadly). This is what I believe we are learning to do. This was the first of many songs that flowed from me from that day on. They came to me without effort and rather than fighting with my inspiration like before, the songs became stronger and deeper. I learned to trust myself and allow the flow of creativity to work through me. This felt like a miracle at work and although I was thoroughly enjoying the process, it took years for me to truly acknowledge what I'd been gifted.

I had now found a voice through my songwriting but it was becoming clear that the lyrics that I would start writing to convey and express my new way of seeing the world were becoming as important as, or even more important than, the music. Little did I know at this time that I was sowing the seeds that would entice the storyteller within me to emerge. This was my way of learning to speak my truth in a way that worked for me. This is something we can all do when we discover we have a voice. Sometimes we simply need to find the right language. I was having no problems finding the words at this time but my confidence in my singing voice was hugely lacking. The first band that formed to perform these songs came into being as Tim, Louise's husband, had received the same clearing as I did. This enabled us to really enjoy the experience together and we were joined by his sister, Emma, from the big band, who introduced me to Louise and Tim in the first place. This band only lasted about a year as we all had different paths and mine was headed towards the harp.

As soon as I bought one in 2003 and began to write songs directly with the harp, I got in touch with an old friend with an extraordinary voice who interestingly had also sung in the party band some years before. I felt she, with her vocal versatility, could work well with my songs accompanied by the harp. For the first time I had faith in what I was offering the world.

It soon became apparent, however, that although my singer's voice was amazing she was having difficulties. Every gig she would have problems with her voice, though only she felt this, and within a year, my singer and I parted company and I began looking for a replacement. Who would sing my songs? People kept telling me I should sing them myself but I knew I wasn't up to it. A few years before I had met a beautiful singer called Lisa Marie, and on our first meeting we had immediately fallen into talking about our journeys. She was a deeply spiritual woman and enjoyed and understood all my ideas, as I did hers. We soon began working together. I had already got a wonderful drummer and bass player on board and the band continued its journey. The following year we began recording our CD and it soon became apparent that there were issues again. Lisa began having problems with her voice when singing my songs and she never seemed to feel on form. She sang on the album beautifully, with her usual professionalism, but I know Lisa would love to have been able to do it all again. I felt I was experiencing déjà vu. I was also having real trouble getting gigs for the band and I was working hard with little success. I hadn't come this far on my journey (it was now 2008) without being able to sense that this just wasn't right. I was losing my flow; something had to give, and of course something was about to.

It was at this time that I took my homeopathic medicine that healed my solar plexus, giving my energy centre a sense of its power. As I took the medicine I felt a shift in my voice. I felt a clearing at my break point in the middle of my voice matching the middle chakra I was healing. However, I knew that this was just the beginning.

In March, when John Wadsworth invited me on his astrology course, on the first Aries weekend there was an evening of performances. I sang a song with my harp.

In the interval a woman came up to me and said, "When did you discover you had such a beautiful voice?"

I must admit I was taken aback. After years of putting my voice down and not feeling confident about myself, I doubted her at first. Then I thought, here am I offering my three skills: my songwriting ability, my harp-playing and my voice, the latter of which I considered the weakest. Now she could have picked up on either of the others but no, she chose to compliment my singing and I must honour that. I graciously thanked her, though part of me was very much aware of how far I could still go with this.

At the same time, I was being drawn to Chloe Goodchild's amazing project *The Naked Voice*. I realised I knew the man who worked for her; it just so happened that it was Tim, and he was wonderful in helping me get on board. At first I went online and hearing her speak of her first experiences, I could feel myself welling up. I knew I had to get involved. When I looked at her list of workshops I realised I couldn't make any till the New Year. This seemed frustrating at first but of course everything is always perfect in its timing and I was learning to relax and enjoy the process. I bought her CD entitled *Your Naked Voice* and began working on her exercises alone, which were very beautiful and expansive.

As the universe was bringing in all these experiences to see if I was ready to embrace them, I was very quickly being shown the very best and worst of my abilities. I felt I was being asked if I was ready to step up to the mark. That summer I happily put myself forward for an open mic evening, something that I have often done, only to be knocked back by finding myself out of my comfort zone. I was confronted by a large audience and sound system. As a saxophonist, I would have been completely in my element. However, as open mic nights offer no preparation time or sound check, as a harpist, I gave possibly the worst performance I have ever played. Soon after I then purposefully put myself out of my comfort zone at a jazz summer school, for reasons I still question, and was gifted a masterclass style lesson that taught me more about my voice in fifteen minutes that I had learned in forty years. It's easy to see what was going on here in hindsight, and when I returned home, the text from Lisa, my singer, bailing out of a gig having completely lost her voice, should have come as no surprise. I was being asked to sing in front of a huge home audience on my own. In my quandary of whether I could do this, a friend offered me some wonderful advice suggesting that I should simply try and get out of my own way and then I'd be fine. It actually worked and I felt a small door open. It is at these points in our lives when we can sense that we are now on our way. Only a little while after, Lisa announced she was pregnant again and would have to leave the band. At first I was devastated but I soon came to see it as part of the flow I was experiencing. *Sing the songs yourself* was still echoing in my ears.

The next gift for me was Chloe Goodchild's voice workshop. It took place on the first weekend of January 2009 in Wales, six months after buying her CD and going to the jazz summer school. Here I met many wonderful people who I now consider good friends. The work that Chloe introduced me to – singing through the chakras, opening and healing them – resonated with me as soon as I had started working with her CD. During the weekend we worked as a community. There were forty of us, singing, expressing, freeing, witnessing and just being. There was a profundity and integrity in the work, but it also allowed for the simplicity of finding joy through song. I also discovered the power of being in a healing space. At one stage I worked in a group of three and we had twenty minutes to be free to just offer whatever sounds we wished. It was initially very challenging but then very freeing once you let go of your own judgement. We each took it in turns to sound, to be the one supporting the one sounding and then just being a silent witness. Whatever role you played, the healing received was the same. It's an amazing revelation and possibly the most important lesson we can learn.

It was soon after this time that I did a home recording of a song I wrote for friends of mine, which was to become my Capricorn song. I asked the friend who engineered my album to transfer this song on to CD for me.

When he gave it back to me he said, "Your voice has improved!"

I thanked him, however, I was beginning to realise that it wasn't my voice that was improving; that was always there. I was now just learning how to stop strangling it, how to relax, stop the critical inner voice and just sing my truth. This was something that hadn't, up till now, felt that easy for me to do. Now I was seeing that through healing my own voice and being given tools to help others find theirs, I was being taken on a far deeper road here.

The joy we can receive when we recognise a completion of a long timeline of unfulfilled emotions can allow the heart to soften and grow more than we can imagine. As I looked back I could see my mother's dreams of being a singer continued through me. My mother did sing and in her middle age accessed enough confidence in herself to go out to perform in old people's homes. As a teenager this was very exciting and I took great pride in her courage and the happiness she gave to so many people. For my mum, however, this was a wonderful hobby; for me I was a musician by profession and my voice was something I was keeping under wraps, knowing it was under par. My saxophone was its replacement and I struggled with that too. I sang in my bands but always as a backing singer. I was blessed to perform alongside some very wonderful singers and somehow I managed to, like a chameleon, take on their qualities as best I could. But my dream was to find my voice and for many years that seemed as though that was how it was going to stay: a dream.

I have, through this experience, learned that dreams carry far more weight than we give them credit for, and I know that this is beginning to be recognised far more widely. If I could have a pound for everyone who, on hearing me play, told me how it was their dream to play the saxophone and now the harp too, I would be a rich woman. These days it is so easy to make this happen but I feel people are slow to recognise that it is their dream for a reason and that it is their duty to fulfil it. Why else would this particular endeavour be their dream?

Helping others to make their dreams a reality is vital because these dreams are our true selves trying to tell us what our purpose on this Earth is, and if we brought it into being we would find so much happiness. I now make it my business to offer anyone whom I sense has lost their voice, through judgement and fear, a way through this with the gifts I have been given. Learning to heal my voice is not about being a star but to simply find joy in the sound that is our own gift to the world, the essence of ourselves manifested. Once we have found the beauty of our own personal vibration it is important that we bring it out into our community and start connecting with others, bringing harmony into the world. The fact that so many words in music are also used to show how we can live in accordance with one another is no coincidence.

It has been a beautiful journey and as I look back over the few years that followed, after having cleared my body of asthma once more and beginning to teach myself to unlearn all my bad breathing habits, I recalled how a woman approached me after one of my solo gigs soon after these events. She said that although she thoroughly enjoyed the gig, she didn't feel I was singing to my best ability. I assured her I wasn't as I felt I was only just beginning my journey, but she also pointed out my awkward posture whilst playing the harp and it dawned on me, for the first time in six years of playing the harp and singing, that the two were pretty incompatible. I realised that as I reached for the strings it was impossible to stand straight. Singing required an open chest, especially after years of shielding my lungs with asthma. I immediately began to wonder how I could overcome this dilemma and I thought of the Alexander Technique. I had read a book on it once many years ago, but that was all.

The following month I found myself at my friend Helen's in Liverpool, checking out the possibility of running a workshop up there. She had invited a friend round for supper and it wasn't long before I discovered he knew about the Alexander Technique, although I have no recollection of how this came up in conversation. I jumped at my chance and asked if he knew of an answer to my problem. When I'd finished telling him of my situation he felt he couldn't offer me any help with the Alexander Technique, however, he went on to explain that he'd just been to the hospital before coming to the meal as he wanted to visit his newborn niece and nephew. He had just been watching them in their incubators, explaining that they were fine, just a little premature, but that they were both lying on their front and breathing as naturally as only a baby can into their backs.

That was my answer – what a beautiful gift of synchronicity. I thanked him wholeheartedly, knowing that by breathing into my back I would solve all the problems of lack of capacity and remove my old patterns as an asthmatic. You can remove the asthma but the old breathing shapes will remain.

As time passed and my voice blossomed I was able to fully enjoy the experience of learning how to find my own voice as something we can all do. Even when it comes at a late stage in our lives it is always perfectly placed and I knew that now I could begin my role facilitating others in how to find their own voice. With so many voices to find, it is important to remember that, although the journey maybe filled with feelings of trepidation, there are no wrong turns, just many paths all reaching the same destination. I would encourage anyone who feels they have not yet found their voice to begin by simply asking the universe and reminding themselves of what their dreams used to be before life got in the way. Once you begin this enquiry there's no knowing where it might take you. Intention is everything and the more people intend to open their lives to all the possibilities they have dreamed of, the more we can bring happiness, fulfilment and variety into this world. Who knows what yet is to be discovered? When someone decides to make a change and seeks their true path, vibrations are sent out into the world enabling others to take up the same baton. I never knew that I could bring miracles into my world until I took a step in the right direction. Once the first step was taken the others simply followed naturally because I was open. Having an open heart is all that it really takes to find your calling, and I know it's catching.

Chapter 10

The High Road

Children of Miracles

A Conversation between Mother and Baby

I hear you, like whispers on the wind.
I hear you, through our roots and through our kin.
I see you, as if your presence weren't enough.
I feel you and your constant love.
Trust me, without words you say.
Trust me, your fear gets in the way.

For we are the children of miracles, the weaver of dreams.
We are the children of miracles, the sewer of seams.

It's easy, living in doubt.
You risk nothing when you leave hope out.
For doubt is the pain that doesn't know that faith is his brother.
And pain is the thing that grips like no other.
Trust me, your young eyes smile.
Trust me, we can go the mile.

For we are the children of miracles, the weaver of dreams.
We are the children of miracles, the sewer of seams.
And we'll make it real, stronger than steel within,
But soft as our skin.

And it's a long road, but we can make it together.
And when we get there, we get to keep the prize forever.

For we are the children of miracles, the weaver of dreams.
We are the children of miracles, the sewer of seams.
And we'll make it real, stronger than steel within.
But soft as our skin.

We have reached the Winter Solstice, the sun is at its lowest point in the sky but we are at the northern point on our journey around the astrological wheel, our midheaven. As we look into the night sky we can see the North Star, Polaris, the centre of our galaxy. This is the point in the sky that stays still while all else spins madly around it. This helps us to find our own inner stillness, our inner wisdom, which can be found as we reach the third eye chakra and the sixth note of the major scale.

A. T. Mann explains how at this point in the womb we take on our mother's reaction to dealing with being pregnant, who she consults to verify her status rather than recognising it for herself and how she broadcasts the news. Whether the parents stress or adopt a more profound understanding of the process affects our philosophy in life.

In life, as we attempt to find a deeper aspect of ourselves, we connect to Polaris as our cosmic source, which we find during the hours of darkness, in the night sky. This reflects the chakra colour we have reached on the rainbow spectrum which is indigo. This contrasts with our journey in Leo where we connected to our conscious source, the sun, which we see in the sky all through our waking hours. We can only get in touch with this deeper energy if we close down our conscious self and look within.

As we begin to journey towards this stationary star, we see the mountain that we have to climb to reach our goal. We have reached the astrological sign of Capricorn, an earth sign once more, which invites us to take to the road on this long, arduous journey. But we are being guided by Saturn, our teacher, our guide, our limiter. However, he limits us in good way. Unlike Jupiter who rules Sagittarius in his expansive way of teaching, Saturn teaches us to find joy in the moment, not to rush; it's not a race. He shows us that by taking our time we can learn each lesson well and reach the summit only when we are ready, making sure we don't run out of steam before we've reached the top. Whenever that time in our life is, we can find that inner wisdom and truly save our soul. This is the time of the Saviour's birth in most northern hemisphere cultures. At the solstice the sun stands still, *sol-stice*, for three days from the 21st to the 24th of December, and then on the 25th it begins its journey northwards. This is the coming of the light, our light, our wisdom.

Often this symbolic journey, however and wherever we take it, needs to place us somewhere quiet so that we can escape this crazy life we have built. This new world, that is getting noisier by the year, is blotting out the silence we need to hear our wisdom. Our cities are getting so loud that those who are not yet ready to take this journey try to cover up the noise with more noise, more distractions and more ways to squeeze more experiences into our allotted time. Headphones, mobile phones, computers on at all hours – people are growing so used to the noise they are becoming terrified of the silence.

For those of us who do understand that a noisy world creates a noisy mind, running to the hills is just where we want to be, even if that is simply about creating a quiet room in our house. When we turn the decibels down a few notches and find the space in our lives to be still, suddenly a whole world emerges that we could never have imagined. Of course, then we have to deal with the constant chatter of the distracted mind that has grown out of the world we had built around it, and it is the third eye chakra that offers this opportunity. By stepping into the stillness within, we find the pearl that lies deep in the core of our brain, the pituitary gland, symbolised by the Hindus as the lotus flower. As the petals unfurl we can reach further and deeper into our truth. This is, of course, not easy and takes much practice and perseverance. So, for most of us, it is never like flicking a switch. It begins with a moment when we manage to create a window and something flashes into our field of inner vision. Like tuning into a radio station, in time, you can get more adept at finding the right frequency. Some find this easier than others; for me it mostly happened when I had my eye off the ball.

Once you have experienced this for yourself a few times then the gifts start to arrive. They can come in many different forms so you then have to work out where your strengths lie. Some people are visual; some receive guidance aurally, others get signs or wonderful synchronicities. Everyone is different, but once you begin to develop your own unique way of connecting then you can use this gift to work towards finding your inner peace.

However, this whole journey is rarely a swift one and it can often bring us to our knees – astrologically, Capricorn is connected to the knees. For some it can be a hard and often painful experience but through the pain, through the suffering, we can learn about ourselves and discover the joy. My song for this month was inspired by my friend and her baby's agonising battle with cancer. As she told me what she believed her baby was telling her, the song simply emerged from the powerful emotions we were all experiencing. I hope the words convey the deep wisdom that the mother felt was gained as she learned to trust and the baby pulled through. As her friend, I could only hold them in my heart all the way.

Culturally, it's this difficult journey, aided by the guiding hand of Saturn – the furthest of the visible planets – which enables us to build structure into our world. As it draws the largest ring around our lives, Saturn represents Father Time and death. What kind of world we create depends on whether we choose to do the inner work or not; whether we create a society of wealth and abundance concerned with just the physical world or whether we include our spiritual well-being as well. That is down to us.

Here we can look at the progression of the three earth signs as Taurus teaches us how to discover our individual feeling of well-being, like the contented Buddha. Virgo brings in the harvest, allowing us to reap the rewards we have worked so hard for as a community. Capricorn creates the wealth and abundance of our community as a human race, which we are now seeing very powerfully as our economy goes global. It can be easy sometimes to get caught up in the negative of each sign, its shadow side. Today we are in a global recession and although it can sometimes seem like we've crawled our way out of it, that could just be the type of illusion the economists are so adept at creating. As their world is built on confidence, by saying that everything is back on track this then does appear to create that state of being. It is interesting how this mirrors the world of affirmation I've been working so hard to build for myself. However, I do feel that until we create an economic structure based on honesty and openness and fairness for all then the economy will continue to struggle. The sticking plaster of a few words cannot cover the gaping wound we have created, and while Pluto remains in Capricorn for the next decade or so it's up to us to make the necessary changes.

It was at this point in the course that I remembered that John had explained in Scorpio, which is ruled by Pluto, god of the underworld, that this planet is taking us through a fascinating journey. As Pluto sits behind the veil it creates a shadow in every sign it enters. In the 1980s Pluto moved into Scorpio, which meant we were about to face the shadow side of Scorpio. Scorpio deals with the taboo, with issues such as sex and death. In this decade we became very concerned with AIDS; a disease that brought these issues together with grim consequences. In the 90s Pluto moved into Sagittarius. Sagittarius is concerned with finding your truth, dealing with religious or spiritual quests, and in this decade fundamentalism became and continues to be the issue of the day. Pluto stayed in Sagittarius until the summer of 2006 when it dipped into Capricorn for a moment and, as Capricorn is all about our global wealth, dealing with its shadow, in that summer we had the Northern Rock bank shakedown. Pluto retrograded out of Capricorn for a bit and everyone thought it was just a blip. It then moved fully into Capricorn in 2007 and we had the full-on meltdown of recession that, if we are honest, I believe we still have today.

I am constantly fascinated by the economic world that we have created, but perhaps incredulous is a better word. As a child, I naively believed that the world was run in a way that was good and true and that when harsh decisions were made it was for the greater good or reasons beyond our control. At fifteen when I was old enough to get a grasp of the way our finances were led I was truly horrified. I felt extremely disillusioned as I began to understand that it was really just a big bookie system.

With the arrival of the new millennium I hoped that this was our chance to make a change. I began to see our economic situation like the Road Runner being chased by Wile E. Coyote. I had that cartoon image in my mind of the coyote running off the cliff, his legs madly spinning, but as he hadn't noticed there was nothing beneath him, he hadn't started to fall. Such was our illusion that everything was still okay. With the changes that came in 2007, I saw this coyote, symbolising the whole human race, looking down and realising his predicament. We fell into recession for a while but then everything seemed to calm down and I believe, continuing that analogy, that we have just caught our shirt on a branch sticking out from the cliff, leaving us hanging in mid-air. With our legs still going, the illusion that everything is fine is keeping us precariously held up by that branch; our economists are using the art of confidence to keep the economy buoyant. However, knowing that this can't last, I have been waiting for the time when the branch will break, causing us to free fall once more. My problem is that I want change so we can start afresh. However, most people are too scared to let go so their fear keeps us clinging to the cliff side. Maybe it's because I've always been a quiet revolutionary and as I said, Pluto is going to remain in Capricorn for some time yet. The fall is not going to be easy but I do believe that what we can create in its wake, the phoenix that will rise from the ashes, will be worth it.

Capricorn, sitting at our astrological midheaven, shows us what we are aiming for in life; our vocation as a race. Personally, I believed my midheaven was in Taurus (there are plenty of astrology Internet sites if you wish to find yours), which meant I was supposed to be aiming for abundance. I'd heard this before. My life as far as the workplace is concerned has never been that arduous nor abundant. Somewhere I was beginning to feel I was missing something.

I have always prided myself on being able to find work outside of the norm. As a teenager, I was teaching, busking and even doing robotics performances at the largest nightclub in town. When I was gifted with my house, this ensured that I would not have to find a full-time job and I could continue with my music, never making much money. I was living on the edge from day to day, and though I was doing okay, I was certainly not abundant.

Although, over the years, things slightly improved, I knew that I still undervalued myself and had a little trouble allowing the energy of attraction to flow easily through my life. In hindsight, I can see that I simply had not found my vocation. When the harp and my songwriting came into my life and I felt at last I had something new and valuable to offer the world, I still felt everything was not quite in place. The problem with my singers and the difficulty getting gigs meant that I wasn't fully in my flow yet. With the onset of 2008, my solar plexus healing and my journey into astrology, things were beginning to turn around for me.

By November I was meeting Chrissy, author of *The Golden City*, regularly and she was looking at my chart and comparing my transits (my astrological chart of the day, rather than of my birth) with the world's transits. They matched perfectly.

"This is your time," she said.

"I know!" I exclaimed. I felt like I was on a conveyor belt at full speed ahead and I had no choice but to stay on it. I actually would have stayed on even if I had the choice to get off; it was the most exciting time for me, the whole year had been a complete whirlwind and it wasn't looking like it was about to slow down.

Later that month I found myself in the staffroom at the private junior school where I taught individual lessons of woodwind and harp, grabbing myself a coffee. This was relatively unusual but one pupil was off school that day so I had a few free minutes. Synchronicity was about to throw me a line and I somehow knew to take it. A part-time job was on offer to cover the music teacher's maternity leave and I just happened to overhear the head teacher, who I just happened to teach saxophone, asking another teacher whether they were interested as no one suitable had applied as yet.

As I listened to the whole conversation, hearing some of the details, something in my mind went into overdrive. I heard the head teacher's voice fall and I knew she'd been turned down.

As the phone call ended, I poked my head around the door and said, "Is this something I might be interested in?" I'm still not sure why I asked as I am not qualified as a teacher at all, let alone a classroom teacher. While everyone else went off to university, I was having a life-changing experience as a member of a rock band in Hong Kong. I had chosen the 'University of Life'.

"Well," she replied, "it's a day teaching music to Years Five and Six, and also teaching religious studies (which I hadn't known about at all until this point) to Year Six, the topic being Judaism." As she finished her sentence her voice went right up as we both realised what she was saying. After ten years with the school and having taught her for two of them, she knew me well enough to know that I was Jewish. The synchronicity of this brief conversation made us both burst out laughing.

Conversely, as the discussions began I also couldn't help thinking seriously if I wanted to take on such a huge task. It was only a day and a bit a week but it was such new territory; it would be doubly hard for me having to learn as I went along. The problem was that it was exactly at this point that I had begun formulating my ideas for *Keys to the Golden City*, an evening of harp, song and journeys. This was very important to me and I knew that it would be something that would grow. Perhaps even then I was aware that I would be doing self-development workshops with it. I knew I would be making a shift from working one-to-one to working with groups and the idea of classroom teaching was kind of a stepping stone to it, but was it too much of a giant leap? Did I need to be taking on something else so huge when I already had my own project in the wings?

Within a week of stepping into the idea of going for this job, I was already trying to step out of it. But on the other hand, I was fully aware that synchronistic events are never an accident. As luck would have it, just before the start of the Christmas holidays I was informed that a qualified music teacher had applied to the school quite out of the blue. For the moment, I felt that I'd been saved.

However, I still agreed to go ahead with the interview at the end of January. By the time the day arrived I had no intention of going for the job. It had been a beautiful moment of synchronicity which myself and the head teacher had thoroughly enjoyed but really, I just didn't have time for it.

I waltzed into the head teacher's office and although I have no real interview experience, I began answering the questions in a confident and relaxed manner, as you do when you have no attachment to something. As I gave ideas for my lessons based on all my past workshop experiences, I began to realise I was putting myself over perhaps a little too well.

Five o'clock came and as I was returning home my mobile rang. It was the head teacher offering me the job. I couldn't find the words to say no and before I knew it I had accepted the post as part-time temporary music teacher. It was an amazing year and although I felt my inexperience I thoroughly enjoyed the whole school performances I was put in charge of and gained great satisfaction from teaching in groups.

It also wasn't getting in the way of my own work. Having spent the whole Christmas holiday period putting together my new performance of *Keys to the Golden City*, it had become quite a project, an hour and a half long with a huge amount of information and of course my songs. The week I started at school, I presented my first performance at the last session of the astrological course, which concerned Pisces; the perfect place for a Piscean to take her first step into bringing all the oneness of her life together in song. The real joy for me was realising the songs had been written before I knew anything about astrology, yet they all slotted perfectly into their astrological places in very meaningful ways. It was as if Saturn had been guiding me all along, offering the structure to gradually bring the pieces of my work together. I was ever thankful.

It seemed strange after the struggle of getting gigs for my band – here I was putting all my effort in my schoolwork and yet my project seemed to be growing like a beautiful seed. It needed little work from me; just the trust that all things grow naturally with the sun's rays.

I had put it out that I wanted a performance a month. They seemed to be coming in so easily and when I did have a gap it would just take a phone call to the right person as long as I kept my heart open and my intentions in the right direction. I was at last swimming downstream and no longer fighting against the tide.

By September, after the gentleness of the school holidays I was ready to return to school and had already set the intention of putting a weekend healing workshop together based on my performance. My next performance was hosted by my new friend, Sue, whom I had met on the Chloe Goodchild workshop, and we arranged to hold it at her house. I decided to ask this audience, as I knew they were all open-minded, kind-hearted and already seasoned travellers on their individual journeys, if any of them would like to be guinea pigs for my new workshop. I was offering a free course in return for allowing me the chance to practise on them, as I was obviously new to this. A few of them began stroking their whiskers gleefully.

It dawned on me that I was, as usual, bounding into this new project of mine without any qualifications; I had never facilitated a healing group before. I needed a practice run in the same way as the astrology course had offered me the chance to try out my performance with the group. However, by this time, after bringing the performance successfully into being and taking on the teaching post without any paperwork or training, I was now fully aware that pieces of paper are often meaningless in the great scheme of things. I remembered how, at eighteen, I had consciously made this decision not to take my studying any further but to get on with living life. Now I felt the need to honour the decision I made at that tender age. It was as if my whole life had been a training ground for this new journey and all the pieces were beautifully in place. I had learned to listen to the guidance and watch out for the synchronicities and recognise their gifts. I didn't have to worry, just be.

In my spare time I began putting my ideas together for each of the twelve archetypal exercises. I needed to make them varied, fun and deep enough to offer a transformation for the participant. This was going to be testing for me but the real lessons were in noticing how I had been gifted with difficult, personal tasks to overcome so I could teach from my own experience. The most important for this course was about finding my voice. The workshop takes all that we have held in separation for so long and connects them in a way that brings understanding and meaning to our lives.

Mother Earth and astrology offer the mechanisms through which we can find balance and harmony in all things, but for me, as a musician, the main key is found in music. However, the keys are different for everyone. Whatever your passion is in life, whether it is cooking, football or study, the list is never-ending, the joy and growth you gain by experiencing your passion is your individual key to enhancing the fulfilment of your life. Yet, I do believe that singing is something that unites us all.

Arriving at the northernmost point on our astrological wheel, this is where we discover our aspirations, our vocation in life. In my mid-forties mine was still not offering the abundance my astrology chart was promising. What was I still missing in my healing journey?

As I stepped into 2010, I tried to set up a trial run of my workshop. However, the snow scuppered my plans and I had to postpone till March.

However, it was in that time that a friend, on hearing one of my mad stories that I'd frequently tell, told me that, "People like to read these kinds of things."

Having just freed myself up from school, as my classroom work had come to an end, and having two months to wait till my workshop could go ahead, I decided to write this book. Realising that I had stories that matched the twelve archetypes, I spent a little time planning the twelve stages and then off I went. By April the first draft was finished and my trial workshop had also been a great success. I'd achieved my creative flow and I was thinking, *Now what?* I set up some workshops but had little response. By the time I had cancelled a few because of the lack of uptake, I was beginning to realise my weekend workshops were obviously offering too much too soon and I was soon getting guidance to put together a shorter three-hour introductory workshop. The response was far more positive. Now I had to think about what to do with the book. It was beginning to dawn on me that again I had leapt without looking. I had rushed into two ventures without truly assessing the situation.

Something wasn't sitting quite right and I began to realise that my midheaven was offering me some signals worth reviewing. It was Chrissy who got it, as she always does:

"You've got an Aries midheaven, that's why you're all fired up about your work."

My time of birth was very loose. My mother told me I was born "before tea." When giving my birth time sometimes I'd vary it slightly, never realising it would make a real difference.

I soon realised that though most charts showed I had a Taurus midheaven, some placed it in Aries. I have a good deal of staying power in my life but as I have my moon in Taurus and my north node, I soon realised I had Taurus already covered.

Having a midheaven in Aries also meant that with the shift in my birth time I had a good deal more Sagittarius in my chart, revealing my constant search for spiritual truths and needing to voice them.

As I reflected on this new clearer vision of myself I recognised the need to use this new awareness of Aries energy in a way that served me, rather than running at things without the necessary preparation.

In August, I managed to find myself involved with the Glastonbury Zodiac book, *Signs and Secrets of the Glastonbury Zodiac. The Maltwood Moot Anthology, Vol. I.* If it was too much to expect anything to happen with my book then a short piece from it was certainly a small, but positive, step forward. The result would take another three years to come to fruition but the beautiful book I was lucky enough to be a part of was certainly worth the wait.

Enjoying the glow of satisfaction I received from this small achievement in my life, I realised that over ten years I had gradually, almost completely, reinvented myself. In contrast to the Aries energy, the Capricorn archetype was showing me that my vocation was going to be a long, drawn-out affair. I was no longer just a saxophonist and teacher but an emerging harpist, songwriter, singer, healer and writer. No wonder I was questioning, when I was thirty, if I didn't have something more to offer. But although I had found my path the world didn't seem interested. If my journey was simply meant to be hard then I could rest with the knowledge that this was my lot, but I knew that I was working towards a state of abundance and my 'poverty consciousness', a phrase coined about me by a new friend, was something I was still in need of healing. My road seemed to be long and winding but my view seemed to be too narrow. I was missing something and I needed to work it out if I was going to move forward.

As the autumn of 2011 came around, a year after my asthma had been healed, I felt another shift. Autumn is the worst time for me as far as my asthma is concerned and as the season changed and the leaves started falling off the trees, my body reminded me that I hadn't completely cleared out my closet. I still had skeletons lurking there. I had peeled away an onion layer, but I had not reached the core. As I looked ahead, though I'd thought I'd reached the top of my mountain, there in front of me loomed another peak maybe even higher than the distance I'd already covered. Maybe we only really reach the top when we die, but I was not going to abandon the ascent even if it meant crawling to the summit.

For now, I decided I needed to widen my point of vision, hoping to find some answers there. I began questioning how we begin to comprehend the climb together as a race, a community. We have so many choices but we can only arrive at the top of the mountain together when enough of us have done the work as individuals and chosen to go the long haul. For the last hundred years the West has chosen to work towards creating a better social system that benefits many if you are strong of heart and mind. If you don't scratch the surface, things could look pretty good compared to before this age of social justice and welfare. However, we all know that once we do scratch the surface things don't look quite so pretty. If we only take care of the physical world, and we're not doing so well at that anymore, then we create a world devoid of spiritual understanding and sanctuary. If we want to truly arrive at the gates of our golden city we have to enter as fully functioning, healthy beings in mind, body and spirit.

I knew that I could only reach my summit and save my soul if I could free myself of all the chains I have brought with me through my life. Although my journey hasn't been arduous, for I have led a blessed life so far, I know I carry with me pain and judgement from my ancestral line that prevents me from truly singing my song. I believe that this is our main objective, to break free and overcome the obstacles that we have built into our culture, preventing us from finding our way home. A new quest was calling me and I knew I had the tools and the understanding of myself to help me on my way, but this would take me on a whole new journey.

In different ways we are all aiming high and doing the work and even though we know we are not there yet, the mountain never stops rising up before us, calling us forth. Each lesson we learn helps us to send that vibration to help others pick it up and run with it. As a unified people we can combine forces and teach each other how to grow and build a world that we all can be proud to live in. However, we also have to remember that we are already there; we have just forgotten this.

If we can open ourselves to the understanding that we are perfect and complete in all we are, we can express and enjoy our knowledge of this through others in celebration of who we are, rather than interacting in a clinging expression of fear. We are learning separation so we can burst out of our shell-like cocoons and come together as complete beings and build our lives in this feeling of wealth and abundance. Remembering to seek peace in our lives will help us hold a steady course.

I hope we can build that understanding of wholeness into our expression of life, and although it is not something one can teach, everyone can experience it for themselves. It is through the hard journey that a place of stillness can be found that opens you up to your inner wisdom. On this path we realise just how much we learn and grow through the experience of sufferance. As we work through the pain and then choose to let it go, great joy is discovered. It's an old cliché but clichés only come into being because their truth is constantly being repeated.

Chapter 11

The Think Tank

Sulha (Reconciliation)

Take a seat at my table.
Though there's blood on our hands, we're like Cain and Abel.
We'll break bread, not our mothers' hearts.
Are we living by the grave or by the cradle?

Sulha, sulha, take a drink with me
Sulha, sulha, a cup of coffee.
Sulha, sulha, take a drink with me
Sulha, sulha, a cup or three.

How should we take our tea?
With a drop of remorse and a lump in our throat.
How should we take our coffee?
We'll keep the dream afloat till we believe in:

Sulha, sulha, take a drink with me
Sulha, sulha, a cup of coffee.
Sulha, sulha, take a drink with me

Sulha, sulha, a cup or three.

And be free of all the rage and all the fear.
And be free, take some time to shed a tear.
And the pain will dissolve like sugar.

Sulha, sulha, take a drink with me
Sulha, sulha, a cup of coffee.
Sulha, sulha, take a drink with me
Sulha, sulha, a cup or three.

We're tying ourselves up in knots inside
We can't eat, we can't sleep, we're like suicide.
We're banging our heads up against the wall,
Just remove one brick and watch it fall,
It's our call, one and all, for:

Sulha, sulha, take a drink with me
Sulha, sulha, a cup of coffee.
Sulha, sulha, take a drink with me
Sulha, sulha, a cup or three.
A cup or three.

As we move into the next month beginning the 21st of January, having reached the top of the mountain at the Winter Solstice we have now saved our soul and we're coming down like Moses from the mount. We have the tablets of stone with the answers inscribed on them and we feel we can now understand how we work and so deal with most problems that come our way. As we look down the mountain at the populace below we can also see how to solve any problems within the group. We see that we are just a reflection of the group as they are a reflection of ourselves. The light that we have discovered within ourselves, we are looking to spark in others. At this time of the year we used to celebrate the Pagan festival of Imbolc, yet few still keep the tradition. This is all about rekindling the flame that we worked so hard to light in Capricorn during the coldest winter months; it celebrates the early signs of spring. However, we are still very much in hibernation at this time as we are formulating how we are going to transform ourselves in readiness for our rebirth in Aries. A. T. Mann shows how at this stage in the womb, our mother begins to develop idealistic attitudes towards motherhood and how she brings these into her world, amongst her family and friends, affects our way of interacting within a group in life.

Arriving at the astrological sign of Aquarius, the water carrier, this is the last of the air signs, with thought processes being at their highest and broadest level, connecting our global community. Aquarius is all about the understanding of the individual working within the community, the part working with and containing the whole.

The song *Sulha* was written to celebrate the work of two wonderful men who, within their community, strive to find peace across warring nations. A Palestinian and an Israeli, they are like father and son and work tirelessly in Jerusalem and across the world showing how it is possible to find reconciliation and love in the toughest terrains if you're prepared to start from the heart and truly understand the situation. They explain how you must work at a tribal level. In the Middle East they work by offering cups of coffee to bring the conversation to the table. If the first is offered and accepted, then talks can begin. After the third cup, the number three having powerful qualities, is offered and accepted, then peace talks are more likely to be successful. Their hard work together with this important metaphor for finding peaceful solutions will be sending its vibrations out into the world, helping us all to change the way we think and live our lives.

It is this problem-solving nature of Aquarius that gave

us the world of science. It was science that gave us the telescope and in 1781 the telescope found Uranus, the first of the unseen, outer planets. This was a revelation and sent shock waves through our understanding of the cosmos, mirrored also by the discovery of electricity, illuminating and revolutionising our experience of life. None of this, I believe, is coincidental. Over the next two hundred years, the telescope found Neptune and then Pluto until in the 1960s science gave us space travel. We were for the first time able to come off the surface of the Earth and see ourselves and how beautiful we are, a revelation that few stop to acknowledge nowadays. In the 1970s we discovered Chiron, the wounded healer asteroid, and I believe that this knowledge has given us a new sense of our place in the world, a new cosmic alignment. Chrissy Philp, in her book *The Golden City*, quotes Haydn Paul's *Revolutionary Spirit* where he talks about the new Age of Aquarius bringing the return of Uranus and his inspirational spirit back into our consciousness. His gifts are being returned to us and as I read this I felt I was coming full circle and revisiting my story about Uranus and the meteor in Chapter 1. I do feel that this is our chance to delve into our collective unconscious and fully embrace it.

It was science that taught us to search for the truth by looking deeper into the physical world, by cutting and dissecting, until we even split the atom. After searching for answers in the separation of all things, I believe the only answers lie in the understanding of the whole. If we are going to problem-solve our way out of possibly the most challenging situation that mankind has ever found itself in, we have to start working together as a community. This is one of the most important aspects of Aquarius. With our ideals heightened, we can learn to love and respect each other and also learn to work alongside Mother Earth, loving and respecting her. With all this talk within our scientific community of connecting web-like threads and the quest for the one theory to unite all theories, the understanding of quantum mechanics and all the unfathomable workings that make up what it is, I am ever hopeful.

For me, the community is where the whole essence of healing can be found. Looking back at our journey, knowing that when the Spanish arrived on the shores of South America, the native Indians there recognised that we were entering a five-hundred-year cycle of disconnecting with our spirit world.

This helps me to see where we are headed. As so many have removed all spiritual connections in their lives, starting with the closure of our monasteries and with many of our churches today empty or converted to individual housing, this has reflected into all aspects of life. Our music, of course, reflecting all that we are, has gradually removed most aspects of spirituality from its content. Indigenous cultures have instruments that use harmonics – the hidden vibrations held within each note that take you to the higher realms – as an important part of their sound. With the age of science and technology we created the piano, along with many other fully chromatic instruments. In order that eight piano keys (an octave) should fit the span of our hand we had to change the slight differences between the frequencies of a sharp and a flat to a uniform frequency. This created meantone temperament and then equal temperament.[1] The upside to this was that we gained the beautiful work of Bach's *Well-Tempered Clavier* to celebrate this amazing invention.

However, as the harmonic frequencies were changed, the relationships between the notes were cut off from each other. Music became concerned only with the fundamental note; the note you can hear. Our connection to harmonics began to lose its relevance in this new world of science and technology we were creating. This, of course, perfectly mirrored our concern only for the third dimension and our denial of the spiritual world. This separation brought us into the world of the individual we have today. Some are now, thankfully, crying out to return to the community in every way and with it, since the 1960s we have been reintroducing the sounds of music from our indigenous culture. World Music has become an important soundtrack to our everyday lives and the indigenous people of this world have been patiently watching us as we go. As I see more people working hard to bring the community back together my heart leaps, as I know the quest is a universal one.

Our Western journey with science has been relatively short-lived, only about five hundred years, yet the Chinese, Egyptians, Greeks, Arabs and many other ancient cultures had already laid much of the groundwork ready for us. Spirituality, on the other hand, has been around since man began its conscious life on Earth. With this in mind, our journey into the world of science has worked miracles in playing catch-up for this very important stage in mankind's history; again, no coincidence there. Similarly it was no coincidence that space travel reached an advanced enough stage in its development to have probes ready to send into deep space when all the planets were aligned perfectly so that it could be thrown like a slingshot off each planet in turn. At no other point in our history did we have the awareness, the scientific knowledge, the finances, the public interest and the planetary alignment to fulfil such a project. Rarely do we stop and acknowledge the amazing uniqueness of that conjuncture of events and all the insights into deep space that it has brought us.

Since the millennium, I became aware that television was showing some amazing programmes connecting all these ideas. The first I remember was a programme discussing links between scientists and those following a spiritual path. What excited me most was a mathematician who often found his inspiration for formulas and his answers from meditation. Many scientists spoke of being simply gifted with insights and often two people at the same time had received the same information on the opposite sides of the world. This, I believe, is no different to channelling and I feel I have also been gifted with visions of the universe, knowing this was offered to me so I could coherently visualise my project for others to be able to understand.

I have always enjoyed gifts in picture form to help me understand the universe. I'm not embarrassed to admit that obviously I need the big-picture, cartoon version but I understand also that it adds a good deal of fun and simplicity to a very complex world. I always felt that those who could explain complex ideas in simple words really knew what they were talking about, rather than needing to hide behind long words. I know my angels work with the utmost simplicity. In my quest to understand how time works I really enjoyed the image of the CD and the different tracks all running concurrently, but it wasn't until I was driving down one of the main streets in my hometown that I saw a simple but beautiful image. It was a barbershop sign, the type that spirals red and white stripes continuously in a seemingly downward motion. This was the continuous, linear, forward motion of time held within a fixed space of the now; the beginning continuously beginning and the end continuously ending. The now never changing. I laughed out loud as soon as I registered it, though I must have seen it a thousand times before.

My understanding of science has always been limited, as I've always put my energies into the arts, but with all these processes going on in my mind, I attempted to educate myself a little. I decided to jump in at the deep end and have a go at reading Stephen Hawking's *A Brief History of Time*. I felt I could translate most of his scientific workings into my way of understanding the universe until, when talking about the

basic laws of physics that govern our universe, he stated that
the laws might have been brought about by God but he thinks
that he is no longer around to influence them.[2]

It was as though he was saying that God had to be present
at the birth of the universe but has since left the building.
This of course is taking the viewpoint of some religions that
God is somehow a separate being from everything else. From
my understanding, God *is* the building. Like a human egg
cell grows to become a human, so the Big Bang expanded
to become the universe, or God, as I call it. I believe it is
God's desire to experience every aspect of life, every colour
of the spectrum that has brought us to this voyage through
this dark night of the soul, this five-hundred or rather five-
thousand-year journey. With the understanding that we have
had to journey far away from home, away from our truth and
full potential in our own heart, we have to come through the
darkest point before we are ready to return. Only then do
we discover it was there in our hearts all along. This is just
a part of our evolutionary story and I believe we are on our
way home; it's just difficult to see the light at the end of the
tunnel as yet.

Hawking also talks about the extra dimensions that
scientists have now discovered, but he states that such are
these dimensions that no intelligent being can reside there.[3]

I feel I have to beg to differ on this point, as I believe that
no physical beings, as we understand the idea of the physical,
third dimension, can reside in these other dimensions but
highly intelligent beings of a higher vibration can certainly
exist there.

I would like to acknowledge that this book was written in
the 1980s and science has changed beyond all recognition
since these ideas were formulated. Not forgetting that it
does hold an important place in our history, this amazing
book also states that scientists have put all their energy into

understanding what and how the universe is, rather than asking why.[4.]

Forgetting to ask why anything is as it is, I believe, is fundamental to our journey. When long-sought-after discoveries arrive in our awareness as a set of figures or equations this removes any concept of meaning in our world. This has led us to a very interesting and maybe difficult place in our world today. As we have strived to understand how the world works by separating it out into tiny pieces, hoping to find answers, in doing so we have removed all the magic and most of our feelings towards the world, leaving us mostly with the feeling of fear. We have discovered a great deal but in never stopping to ask why or indeed if such roads should be taken, we have ignored the world of cause and effect, of karma, as scientists only look at the single road and fail to view the whole map.

As the medical world struggles to find cures for an ever-increasing host of diseases, our fear and single-track, rather than holistic, methods mean we just create more problems with the cures we administer. As we spend more and more money on research, drugs and expensive and invasive operations, I feel we're missing a huge opportunity here. To bring back the question 'Why?' into our lives, to understand ourselves on every level, particularly the emotional, we can begin heal aspects of ourselves crying out to be reconciled within us all and prevent dis-ease in so many areas of life.

For me, some of the positive signs are showing themselves as now some scientists are beginning to rethink their view of the world. Many now also believe in God and feel that this is compatible with their understanding of science. I hope that with this they may come to an understanding that in asking the question 'Why are things as they are?', much more could be understood. My optimistic outlook enables me to believe this will happen and with it a more beautiful way of living on this Earth, of loving, respecting and fully understanding her workings, will become apparent.

As I continued to watch more documentaries I felt I was being shown how the scientific world was continuing to open up before our eyes. A documentary I watched about Stephen Hawking's life explained how his physical disability meant that he worked less with formulas and more with concepts and images. It became possible to imagine how it was his illness that enabled him to see the world in a way that no one else could see it.

Hawking's investigation into understanding black holes, and other scientists who have joined the quest, have created a theory that states every being holds its information in the form of light at the edge of its domain. For a black hole, this would be the event horizon, and as I understand it, for humans it's our auric boundary and this, of course, works for the universe also. The light acts like a hologram projecting its image to the centre to create the physical being itself. We are that holographic projection, as is the whole universe. This beautifully mirrors how healing works, travelling through the chakra layers, expanding our consciousness to the edge of the universe. The answers are all there and when we make the necessary changes on this vibrational level this automatically transforms the physical dimension, one being a holographic reflection of the other.

Scientists have difficulty explaining this phenomenon. They know they can describe the universe in mathematics but the quantum nature of what goes on in the higher dimensions makes it difficult to explain or even make sense of in words.

Knowing that many scientists are obviously struggling to bring logic into this new way of thinking, those of us not caught up in linear mindsets can see that this is where the magic happens. It is our faith in a world beyond our dimension, and possibly our comprehension, that enables us to embrace its findings; or not. For the scientific community this is clearly very challenging but for the general public, I believe, the way out of this dilemma would be to let go of the intellectual need to understand these new truths and to simply know it in our hearts. Not an easy task for the logically orientated mind, but I also believe that letting go of the limiting nature of logic may be a way forward. There are, of course, some scientists able to make this dimensional leap.

It is the masculine, straight-line energy of the eye that scientists use which was handed down to us by the Greeks. Yet many people, like Edward de Bono, show that when you use the feminine spiral energy of the cochlea in your ear, you discover there are many roads and many truths that can be found by investigating many different directions. Why only investigate A to B when A to C or D or E etc. might throw up equally positive answers? Of course our business world creates financial and time restrictions preventing our scientists from truly fulfilling their work. If we could transcend these limitations and discover that more options were available to us, we could choose the most appropriate truth to follow, based on its meaning in our world. Maybe we would then be able to keep to a code that served humanity as a whole rather than the few.

It is important to remember that the Greeks did also offer us the positive custom of putting their understanding of the world into stories. Having forgotten to uphold this tradition we have lost the mechanism that puts meaning into our lives and keeps us on track.

When I wrote my first *Plum Tree* story and gave it to Chrissy Philp to read, the first thing she said was, "Well done, you've put your ideas into a story, people like to read stories."

As science offers us more and more technology that encourages us to rely more and more on images outside of our minds we begin to lose our ability to create stories for ourselves, limiting our connection to ourselves, our imagination and so our personal power.

The door that led to finding my story had been closed for so long it would take many different attempts to open it and begin to remember where I had come from. When I began my healing journey I realised I had lost all connection with my higher self, as I did not even know such a thing existed until this point. Wanting to find a way to reconnect, I attempted some channelling. Using a pendulum was, and still is, a very powerful tool when it came to asking my higher self for 'yes' or 'no' answers. Sensing that this wasn't enough, I also tried an alphabetic system, using the pendulum to spell out words, letter by letter. You can imagine that this could be a particularly slow and laborious method, and after a couple of years, my lack of patience and confidence put an end to it. I remember the last time I gave this system a try was sometime in 2002. Sitting on the edge of my bed, I was almost goading my spirit guides, who, as I have said, I affectionately call 'them upstairs', and asked if they would give me something I had never heard of before. Previously, whenever I channelled anything, I always tended to doubt where it had come from, thinking I might have just created the words myself and projected them through my pendulum. So here I was asking for proof that I wasn't just 'making it all up'. I started swinging the pendulum. What I wrote down, letter by letter, was *red alpha waves*.

Red alpha waves. What did that mean to me at the time? Well, I'd heard of alpha waves but didn't know what they were, and I'd never heard of them being put together with a colour before. So with one eyebrow raised, I left it at that. As I do with anything I encounter and cannot make sense of at the time, I put the information into storage until a possible time when something might come along to help me. Then I put my channelling with the alphabet system back into its box, where it has remained ever since.

Six years pass and I'm attending my first meeting held by Tareth, an incredibly powerful man, who manifests the silent vibrations (silent to our ears anyway) of the Earth into audible sound. He also manifests oils and has recently begun to manifest light as well. This was the end of 2008 whilst I was formulating the first stage of my *Keys to the Golden City* project. Linking this with my new work with Chloe Goodchild, putting musical notes alongside our chakras – which I had always associated with colours rather than sound – I was beginning to ask about the connection between light and sound and their frequencies. At this meeting in Glastonbury, Tareth played recordings of sounds he had manifested at Avebury stone circle, and also showed pictures of images that had been created from these sounds by a sound-to-light machine. The sound was utterly amazing and the images were very beautiful, consisting of dodecahedrons and pentagons. These shapes, and their equivalent numbers of five and twelve, resonate very powerfully in all sacred work; in geometry and numerology, astrology and music. The synchronicity was perfect.

The following day, I thought I'd try the Internet. Of course, there were many relevant sites. One in particular caught my eye. It showed the full colour spectrum with the frequencies of light and sound mapped alongside each other. This was a wonderful beginning, and the numerical links between the frequencies were very clear. I was not particularly surprised to find such links; it was just that I had not been aware of anyone making these connections before now.

Soon, I began to sense that it is a spectrum, starting with the dense, lowest frequencies of matter. As the frequencies increase, the spectrum moves from matter to rhythm, with its long frequency waves, represented by our outer planets, producing a sound like a bass drum. As we travel through to the higher frequencies of our inner planets they create the faster beats like a snare and high hat, a whole drum kit, in effect. As the frequency of the beats increase, they seem to merge into one continuous note. Here, rhythm turns to sound, and as these frequencies all form part of a numerical series, this sound is also music. We also encounter radio and microwaves and the whole spectrum of brain waves as the frequencies increase towards the speed of light, represented by our sun, starting with the visible through to the very highest gamma waves and beyond.

As I looked a little further down the page of the Internet site, I noticed the words *alpha waves*, and there in front of me was the colour spectrum, with the colour red very clearly shown. This was the first time I had seen these words connected to colour, and the words *red alpha waves* immediately came back to me. I hadn't thought of them for six years.

The following month we reached the astrological sign of Aquarius and, as part of the Alchemical Journey, were invited to walk the Aquarius figure of the Glastonbury Zodiac with Anthony Thorley. He is an inspiring authority on earth and sky relationships, walking and working with this landscape zodiac in particular. This involved climbing Glastonbury Tor. John had asked me to meet up beforehand with a few others on the course, since he wished to film testimonies of our experience of the Alchemical Journey as it was drawing to a close. As the cameraman was setting up his camera to film me playing my harp, we began talking about the healing abilities of vibration and how some hospitals were actually beginning to use harpists in the operating theatre.

It appears that doctors are becoming increasingly aware of how the powerful resonance of the harp enables a reduction in the amount of anaesthetic needed. This was, and still is, very exciting to me, and I have begun to offer my harp CDs to those who are interested in this kind of healing work.

As we began the walk, the cameraman was carrying his huge camera on his shoulders and I was commiserating with him on having to lug it up the Tor. Then I said, with a big grin, "You know, in a few years you won't need that thing at all. We'll all be telepathic."

He laughed and went on to tell me that experiments in telepathy are being conducted. He explained that people are put into red rooms and encouraged to think of others they know and connect with them. Then he said, "You know, they connect by alpha waves."

I nearly fell over. Over six years had passed since I received the channelling, and within the space of one month I'd been gifted two beautiful pieces to my puzzle which brought me to the understanding that alpha waves in a red environment can enable telepathic communication. It began to dawn on me that, having asked my guides for a piece of information that I'd never heard before, they were giving me exactly what I'd asked for. Not only were they genuinely communicating with me (remember, I had never heard of red alpha waves before), but they were also telling me *how* they were communicating with me: via red alpha waves. Knowing that I love this kind of thing, I was beginning to realise just how much they were humouring me. It was as if I'd been given a cryptic puzzle that took me six years to complete.

The more I thought about this, the more I realised the puzzle had been thrown at me a good deal earlier. When I was in Hong Kong in 1986, on the day we left for Singapore, we were sent a letter from someone who we'd been talking to in the club in which we played. The letter contained an essay about the journey of man's communication in relation to the human brain. Only now, as I'm writing this, I am suddenly aware of how this relates to Chrissy Philp's *The Golden City*, which uses the human brain as a map of the cosmos. The essay explains that mankind learned to communicate, developed the wheel, and then as roads became the main form of communication, we went on to discover the telegraph, the phone and the television. As this was 1986 the Internet was not mentioned in the essay, however, it did suggest that we would soon have mobile phones. This was described as a mirror of the development of the brain; as we learn and grow the cells slowly connect until we become fully communicating beings. In this way, it explained, we would then become telepathic.

To me this made no sense. I couldn't see how by diving further and further into the technological world we would gain the ability to read each other's minds. My feeling was that technology was preventing our extrasensory abilities from flowering rather than aiding them. However, as always I stored the information hoping I would find an answer to this conundrum. Twelve years later when I began my healing journey, the first book I read in the mind, body, spirit field was *The Celestine Prophecy* by James Redfield. Within the first few pages my problem was answered. He told the same story of how we are getting more and more involved in our technology but he explained that when we reach the this new age – the astrological Age of Aquarius – we will hit a wall, throw the technology away and become telepathic. Here I was now, eleven years later, hearing again how all these pieces are beginning to fall into place. So this was actually a twenty-three-year puzzle, but as I'd learned in Capricorn, it's not a race. But with our growing understanding of all this it is up to us to use our scientific findings in a way that works for our society as a whole. I am confident science is beginning to reflect this.

We started to climb the steep incline to the Tor and I found myself in the company of a man called Hugh, who wasn't actually on the astrology course. The contemplative walk had been opened up to a wider circle of friends, and in fact the people in the Alchemical Journey group were the newcomers. Attached as I was at the time to my asthma, I made a comment about how well I felt I was doing, as I was getting close to the top without a single wheeze or cough. Hugh immediately began telling me about his newfound passion, Theta Healing, and how he believed it could help me. The more he told me about it, the more interested I became, primarily because of the synchronicities that were unfolding but also because it seemed to sit well with my desire to see science and spirituality brought together.

As we were coming down the Tor, I began excitedly telling my revelations to the only Aquarian on the course, knowing he'd enjoy my story, from the red alpha waves to the telepathic experiments through to the Theta Healing. I wasn't expecting any more information at this point, but then he started explaining further about all the different kinds of waves – alpha, beta, delta, gamma and theta – and which brain function corresponds to which wave form.

I could feel the smile on my face broaden and my inner glow deepen as it always does when you begin to recognise the joy of these moments and what's really going on. I'd thought I'd barely opened a door, but it felt like I'd opened floodgates. It seemed like every step I took was bringing me more and more exciting information.

Well, we were at the top of Glastonbury Tor, on the Aquarius figure of the zodiac. I had only learned the day before how Aquarius is linked to science and is ruled by Uranus, which was discovered at the same time as electricity, sending a bolt of energy into our lives. And here I was, in the midst of my Uranus opposition, receiving a whole series of energising revelations.

Then I remembered an evening about seven or eight years previously, when I'd been attending a crystal healing group. Usually there was a guided meditation, and on this occasion, I remember being guided to see an orb with the sign of Gabriel's cross of peace on it. Instead, I saw the Earth with a tuning fork connected to it by its two prongs; in a sense, upside down. This was very early in my work with sound healing, and though I didn't fully understand it at the time, it was quite a revelation to me.

Then in 2009, at another meeting with Tareth, he explained that he believes that at sacred sites such as Avebury or the pyramids, the ancients used the stones as conduits for the sound, like a tuning fork. I was at last seeing the connection.

Realising that a tuning fork viewed as I saw it is also the shape of a human with two feet connected to the ground, I was beginning to see that this was something we can all do, when we're ready. Here I was at Glastonbury Tor, one of the most sacred sites in the world, and could see that the tower at its summit was also shaped like a tuning fork, meeting the Earth exactly as I had seen it in my visualisation.

Eventually, I did go to Hugh's ThetaHealing group, where he told me he had felt very guided to help me that day. It was a connection that led to a whole new set of pathways. I learned how when we are in our normal state of being, our brain uses beta waves to function. When we meditate or go into a deeper state of consciousness, we are using alpha waves. Theta works at an even deeper level, the level where all healing is possible. As we expand our consciousness to fully reflect the whole cosmos, amazing things can happen.

These visits led to my enrolling on Tracy Holloway's three-day course where I learned the basics of the healing methods, and met Cathy, who gave me that wonderful psychic reading that helped me unlock some of my limiting thought beliefs. The sound healing course, led by Tareth, where I saw Cathy's vision of the two horses was held within view of the Glastonbury Tor. He finished the day by manifesting the sound out of a crystal. I had already heard his recordings of manifested sound at Avebury and the Great Pyramid in Egypt; however, this was the first time I had heard the sound directly in his presence. It felt like I was witnessing a miracle, and it was one of the most beautiful things I have ever heard. As he turned the crystal in his hand, all the filaments, like high-pitched crystal bowls, were chiming and exquisitely singing together.

The sounds that I heard from this crystal and sounds that we all make silently and unknowingly are all based on the harmonic series, frequencies held within each note which take us from the audible sound, the third dimension, to the higher realms. This is a beautiful journey however we choose to take it. The more we get in touch with it and allow it to heal our own individual inner vibration, the easier and more joyful our life can be. Then maybe this knowledge will be more widely accepted as truth as we become more willing to heal as a community.

As I try to bring all these ideas together, I feel that we are arriving at the last few pages of the story *The Alchemist*. We are on our way home to discovering our true heart and that it was always there. As I had come from a place of knowing there was something lacking in my life, I could recognise the feeling of discontent within our community as we constantly look at others to see what is missing in ourselves. Unlocking the door to the new gifts I had to offer showed me that if we were all taught how to find our own hero's journey we would understand that we all have a gift in life and how to find it. Even if it may seem small, that gift is a perfect piece of the jigsaw that, when joined with everyone else's, creates the society that works for the good of all.

Understanding the Schrödinger's cat theory,[5] that what you see depends on you; makes you not just the observer but the participant. We can create our life depending on what we choose to see. If you think there is magic in the world, you will find magic. If you think there is joy, you will find joy. If you decide there is no God then you will find no God. We are our own creators, made in God's image; a reflection of the first point of existence that became the whole universe. We are all from that first atom and we have the power to create beyond our wildest dreams. We just have to release the fear and choose to vibrate at the highest frequency we can.

In my eagerness to get to this place I feel it is important that we choose to remove any judgement and begin to recognise that there are many paths that can take us to our destination. We can see how many who lose physical faculties in life often gain great inner wisdom. Similarly, some physically well people choose to spend their lives sat in meditation to get closer to their understanding of God and make little use of their bodies. We are all being offered experiences of limitation, individually and as a whole, to discover great expansion at some point in our lives and what we do with that is up to us. But to understand that everyone has a journey, a story of their own, is so important for personal happiness. Though each path leads to the same door, it is important to remember that we, whilst we're in this illusionary state of separation, are all varied in many beautiful ways. Reconciling the differences whilst remembering to discover the unity that binds us all together is why we're here.

When we fully appreciate this we can start bringing people back into our community whom we, at the moment, believe do not fit into the boxes we expect everyone to live by. We will see how everyone can play their part and learn to be a teacher as well as a pupil. Then everyone can be embraced into society without judgement, for who truly has the right to judge? When we can understand the concept that we are all connected and we all carry the best and the worst of what we see in our world within us, then our community can lift itself up and coexist in harmony. We can all celebrate as the individual heals themself completely and reflects this into the community as a whole and our beautiful Earth. Only then can we enter the gates of the golden city as one, as that is what we truly are.

Chapter 12

The Release

To Music

Are you awake now? Seems you've been asleep for years.
The mist is rolling away like falling tears.
You've been listening, you had the radio on.
While the angels were singing, did the cat get your tongue?

Here I am though I never went away.
You got lost in the techno like feet stuck in clay.
Don't stop your singing and I won't stop mine.
You need your voice like the fisherman needs his twine.

Ooh, I am the sound of the spheres.
Ooh, I bring you joy, I bring you tears.
Ooh, I am the sound of the spheres.
Ooh, I bring you healing through the years.

You sing, you feel better.
We sing, we feel good inside.
We all sing, and nations together

Feel the love they can't deny.

Ooh, I am the sound of the spheres.
Ooh, I bring you joy, I bring you tears
Ooh, I am the sound of the spheres.
Ooh, I bring you healing through the years.

Can you hear voices singing? It's the dawning of the day
Can you hear them singing? They're showing the way.

Ooh, I am the sound of the spheres.
Ooh, I bring you joy, I bring you tears.
Ooh, I am the sound of the spheres.
Ooh, I bring you healing through the years.

Here we are, almost at the end of our journey; the buds are preparing to burst through from the void as winter draws to an end and the baby is preparing to leave the watery cocoon of the mother's womb. Spring is near and there is a stirring in our heart as we sense the new beginnings on the horizon. We are at the twelfth and last stage of the wheel and hopefully have all our chakras open.

This sign brings us to the last of the seven chakras, the crown chakra, where we gain knowledge of the highest aspect of ourselves; we are in touch with the angel that is working with us and is the spiritual essence of who we are. To find this connection we have to immerse ourselves fully in the big, deep, watery ocean that is Pisces – the oneness. We can connect all our chakra energies together in a big bowl of light, our egg-shaped, womb-like aura. As each chakra contains all the chakras below it within its energy, like Russian dolls, so this sign contains all the energies of the previous astrological signs within it. It is the universal energy of the one and here we can find a state of living in grace.

This is the last of all the signs, but also the last of the water signs, and we can reflect on this journey as the first water sign, Cancer, allows us to reconnect emotionally with our past, our inheritance. The second, Scorpio, allows us to connect psychically with the beings that are working around us and sensually with those in our lives, and the final stage of Pisces enables us to reconnect with all the energies, unseen, past, present and future. As we remember that all is one – energy, time and all the dimensions of the whole cosmos – we can be released, with immense gratitude, into this universal flow.

The two fish that make up the constellation of Pisces are thought to be Eros and Aphrodite, the god and goddess of love, that turned themselves into fish to escape the monster Typhon (also understood to be a typhoon). Held together by a cord, so they wouldn't lose each other, they are tied with a knot, the star Alrisha. It is believed this star moved from the edge of the constellation Aries to Pisces around two thousand years ago, signalling the beginning of the Age of Pisces with the birth of Christ, the Saviour. Today the fish is used as a Christian religious symbol. In the sky, one fish lies horizontally and the other reaches upwards.

A sign of high aspirations, karma and release, there is great sacrifice as the mother prepares for the last stage of pregnancy. Her willingness to accept this can offer us the understanding of true spiritual values in life. In recognising that the ego often has to step down for the greater good is where we begin to grow, and parenthood is the greatest teacher here.

The strong symbol of our duality is keenly felt in this sign. We are always looking to better ourselves in all walks of life but the spiritual values are very present in this archetype. The need to stay grounded throughout this process of self-improvement is vital; to keep ourselves rooted to the Earth and its gifts. We saw how this can go wrong in the 1960s when we had the great spiritual movement in the West. As this teaching was absent the idea of reaching higher mental states by taking mind-expanding drugs soon became more important the spiritual destination itself. The movement's foundations caved in and it has sadly left a misconception in the minds of many of what true spiritual growth actually means.

The shadow side of this archetype, as its ruler is Neptune, hidden behind a great gaseous cloud, gets lost in the haze. When Neptune was discovered in the 1800s we had the Impressionist movement in art and all the images became blurred, and music became very discordant with the music of Debussy in particular. The beauty in all the arts was inspirational but behind it all was the arrival of the opium dens, and as disillusionment took the place of enlightenment, the dark side of this aspect of ourselves was revealed and then reappeared in the 1960s.

Believing, as I do, that we are being given another chance to lift ourselves into a higher state of being, we need to learn the lessons that we have previously ignored. Staying healthy in our physical body becomes paramount.

This final stage brings us to the seventh note in the major scale and if you sing up the seven notes of this scale you will soon realise that you can't stop there. You have to finish, or resolve it and return home to the octave, the eighth and last note in the scale which is the same note as the first. Like the *Aum*, we realise that the end is also the beginning, it is continuous, and although Pisces is the end of the astrological and seasonal year, it is also part of a cycle and flows naturally into spring without a pause for breath, just like the clock that doesn't pause before returning to the first hour of the day or the first minute of the hour.

On the other hand, as we now know there is only the present moment, continually offering us time to stop and reflect. So as I pause to contemplate our twelve-stage journey that we revisit every year of our lives, I am aware of the seven chakras that we have experienced and the seven notes of the major scale, with the eighth note that resolves to the first note again, but an octave higher. This relates to the image of our life journey as a spiral: the fact that we begin our life at source, a point in space and time, but with each cycle of the seasonal year we travel further out from that point. So each year we return to the same place on our radial cycle, our ascendant, our orbital return, but each year we find ourselves spiralling further out from the beginning point, our birth. Each year we raise our vibration, symbolically, by an octave. An interval of an octave gives us the first two notes in the harmonic series.

The fact that we have experienced seven chakras and seven musical notes is important because actually we have five more chakras, the others being found within our auric field, which can be brought into play should we wish to raise our vibration even higher, gaining more keys to our golden city. Similarly, in music there are twelve notes in the chromatic scale. The stem of the prefix 'chrom' comes from the Latin word for 'colour', i.e. the full colour spectrum. If you think of the piano where the notes are laid out clearly you can see the seven white notes of the scale and the five black notes lying in wait, in the void, should one wish to raise the vibration to a higher key. If you are in C major and wish to modulate, using musical terms, to G major, the next key on the musical cycle, you simply bring the sharp at the seventh step into play to raise the vibration of the music. You can continue in this way through all the twelve keys. It's these five states of being, the chakras held within our aura and the sharps or flats, that are the quantum world, the unseen higher dimensions.

One of the most beautiful and fascinating books I have been introduced to, Joachim-Ernst Berendt's book *The World Is Sound: Nada Brahma*, brings this image into flower for me even more beautifully as he compared this information to the study of music reflected in our cellular make-up. Two scientists have been working on this idea, the German musicologist Wilfried Krüger and the French nuclear physicist Jean E. Charon. There are many different types of scales and many different types of cells but here Berendt relates the major scale to the oxygen atom. He explains how the atom contains eight electrons and protons and how the positive and negative spins of the particles exactly match the C major scale with the negative spin, relating to the semitone, lying at the fourth and eighth steps of both the scale and the nucleus. He goes on to say:

The concurrence between the microcosm and harmonics becomes even more astonishing when one notes that the model of the nucleus of the oxygen atom with its protons has twelve steps, the exact number of intervals found in the scale formed by the atomic model. In the normal state, seven of these intervals are filled and five empty, just as the intervals are in the musical scale of seven "regular" notes, leaving the other five unused. It does happen in music, especially in the process of modulation (change of key), that these five "irregular" notes are employed; precisely the same thing happens during the various saturation states of the atomic nucleus, although these have only a transitory function – as does modulation in music.[1]

There has been a good deal of study in this area, Pythagoras being one of the first that we know of to dedicate much time to this subject and leave us with written documentation, yet none of it had been taken seriously in the science world. Only perhaps recently is it being considered by the few but it will obviously take a while to filter through and become an accepted common truth. Quantum physics has taken a hundred years to become part of our language so I'm not expecting overnight miracles. Yet on the other hand I am – this is a time of great change and great understanding and I believe the balance can be tipped very easily, and when truth is understood clearly it spreads like wildfire. I do feel change will come from the individual working within the group, the coming together of the thinking Aquarian working with the feeling Piscean; once one drop of water is released it quickly connects to the whole ocean.

To me, Berendt's theory answers so many of my questions: the fact that we are sound. The vibration held within everything is sound, and so is music. We are silently singing and so is everything from every living being to every rock and planet. When pupils ask me why music is as it is, why do we have scales and notes and intervals, in the past I couldn't really answer, I'd just say that was how it was created and formed. Now I feel I truly understand that music wasn't created, as such, it came about as a direct reflection of what is within us; it is the manifestation of our silent quantum world and our cellular make-up.

There has been some study into the harmonic structures within our cosmos. The idea that there is a mathematical correlation between the distances of the planets from each other, giving a divine order and a musical structure to our world, has been held in doubt for millennia. It seems quite clear to me that the truth found in these suppositions would entirely depend on the person receiving the information. Some will see a correlation and others will not, as with the Schrödinger's cat theory. The truth depends on the interaction of the person viewing it, as there is the belief that everything is relative, including truth. I believe the universe was created using the first two dimensions of light and sound; in the beginning was the word and then God said, "Let there be light." In order that I can be effective as a sound healer, I work on the basis that all things vibrate, creating light and sound, the music of the spheres. This is reflected in all things down to the very electrons in our bodies, and brings us all together beyond the physical world.

The importance of sound in our culture is something

I believe we used to understand. Jill Purce, in her talk *The Healing Voice*, explained how surviving artwork in the form of stained-glass windows, from before our extreme world of separation kicked in with the Renaissance, showed angels all with their mouths open, singing. As they silently sang to us, we would sing back. This was a beautiful and important exchange, which we seemed to have deemed no longer important in this modern age. When you sing you heal your vibration and so start to heal all aspects of yourself. This was always understood and done without thought. We can then sing with our family and heal our place within our family. Now modern living has changed the way we exist in our homes, with separate rooms and separate musical devices. But before these shifts, families would entertain themselves all together. We would also sing with our community and church. Here we would heal our community and our place in that community.

I wrote the song *To Music* to celebrate this understanding of music in the widest sense of the word. I wanted to convey the idea that music isn't just about performance but also about healing. In the lyrics I use music, in the first person, telling us we have just been listening and forgetting to sing. It is now time to remember this and the demand for choirs and the desire to reclaim our voices is evident, thank goodness.

Although I keep talking about music being the most important aspect of life for me, I need to step into a bigger ocean again and remember that of course love is the container for all. If sound and light are the first two dimensions, these are the basis of our duality. The unifying state comes from the love energy, which contains everything within it. The healing nature of this energy is unquestionable and when the Beatles sang *All You Need is Love* in the first worldwide satellite broadcast, I think that was the most perfect message.

I know people laugh and say, "Well, you know love won't pay the bills!" I believe they're still living in the world of separation and fear. When you are truly living in the flow of life, giving and receiving love and working with positive guidance, all your needs will be met. It needs to be understood, however, that we are talking about needs and not greed.

The most real experience I was gifted with to help me understand the importance of this vibration in all its glory happened in 2003 on the eve of purchasing my harp, the experience I touched upon in Libra.

It was Midsummer's Eve and the first pleasant one in what seemed like years. We were travelling up to a particular shop in Bradford to find a harp for myself and a hurdy-gurdy for Andy. We stopped at a beautiful campsite outside Tewkesbury and the sunset looked like it was going to be amazing. We got stuck in for a night of stargazing and talking and though the sun never really set – it hovered just below the horizon line – as it began to rise the real show began.

For me it was a constant flow of images with the sky moving through the rainbow colour spectrum and the clouds creating the pictures. I tried to keep an account of what was happening but all I had on me was a paper napkin. I have kept this as a memento; it has all the shapes and words that I scrawled down in an attempt to hold on to all that occurred. I think I was worried that I might forget it but as I sit here writing, many years later, I have no need to try and dig it out to jog my memory; the memories and images are as clear as if it happened yesterday.

The first cloud formation, on my left, was a huge robin sitting on a branch and its body was a dull grey/brown colour, as clouds are when the sky is semi-dark. However, the big, red sun was just peeking its head over the parapet so his breast was a vibrant red. On the right-hand side of my vision, or screen, as it felt, was a cloud shaped like a huge angel flying in horizontally to meet the robin. This flight was obviously in slow motion but with patience, I watched them slowly come together and kiss.

The sky became redder and as the sun rose fully the colours moved through to orange and yellow and the dance of the sun on the clouds was so beautiful it wasn't long before I burst quietly into tears. It was a gentle flow of pure pleasure and gratitude. As the green gave way to the bright light blue I was aware that there had been a light layer of mist over my head, which the sun was now burning off. For years after I had been describing this mist as a veil and it took quite a while for me to realise the significance of the bridal veil that pre-empted what was to come. Soon all that was left was a twist of cloud slowly turning, caught in a gentle eddy of wind, like a huge chakra, which now appeared to look like a bunch of flowers.

The bunch of flowers appeared to be spinning very slowly in the sky and then each individual flower became an angel standing on a pedestal, and each pedestal was standing on a scallop shell. This is the symbol of the pilgrimage and also the journey to the fifth dimension. My eyes were drawn to the central figure. She looked to me like a Greek goddess, the most beautiful woman with dark flowing hair. It wasn't till I visited Louise later that week that I learned that was my higher self; at this point I was content with the knowledge that this beautiful energy seemed to be connecting with me. Next to this image, to the right, was the earthly counterpart and I saw what appeared to me to be an old court of law, with large oak benches and a high, raised bar for the judge. Here I could only see a gentleman who was in full Jacobean dress. I could see everything from his long, dark, curly wig to the buckles on his shoes. He was going to be my messenger.

I did actually stop at this point and question what I was seeing. I often make shapes out of clouds, we all play that game, but this was unreal, the clarity and detail was so intricate. What I discovered I could do, if I chose to, was to switch off the mechanism that was making this vision so elaborate and just look at the cloud shapes for what they really were. I could then switch it back on and it was if someone had placed a piece of clear acetate over the top with all the back outlines of the detail drawn on it. It reminded me of how cartoons used to be made. This control I had did not seem to perplex me at the time but looking back it seems quite amazing. It was also confirming the idea that I always seem to get the cartoon version of any channelling that's being offered.

As I was able to take in both scenes the meeting of the higher dimension suddenly took on a bit of a twist. For one turn only my beautiful angel turned into a *Shrek* ogre version of herself. My eyes almost popped out of their sockets, if they weren't already on stalks, and then she returned to normal. There was no explanation and at that point I can't really remember how it made me feel, other than that this was all very bizarre. You must remember that in 2003 *Shrek* was very 'of the moment'. You might think that angels belong to eras past, but I know from experience that they only work in the now. They know how to push your buttons and if you're quite a serious person, like me, they know how to make you laugh.

After a few moments, a few more turns, the image fell apart before my eyes and the angels were falling away. My first reaction was *Oh my goodness, what's happening?*, but the words came very clearly to me: *Don't worry, the meeting is over, that's all.*

With relief I looked at my watch; it was nearly five in the morning. Andy had gone to bed some time ago and I desperately needed sleep for the day ahead. So I climbed into my sleeping bag and closed my eyes. Not so fast – I quickly realised it wasn't over yet. The messenger was coming to give me his message. After all I'd seen, I couldn't sleep now.

My head suddenly exploded with sound, it was like there was a party going on in there. Many voices were chattering away and I got the sneaky feeling they were all laughing at me, but in a kind, well-meaning way. It was not what they were saying, for at first it was just a blur of sound, but what

I could pick out was that they were all talking in Bristolian accents. Now I don't have one myself but I have lived in Bristol all my life and can certainly pull one out of the bag when I need to.

When I first had my awakening, five years before, one of the first books I read, offered to me by my friend Seb, was channelled by the Pleiadians. They are renowned for having a great sense of humour and I got a feeling that they were here with me now. The first phrase I heard which came clear as a bell out of the hubbub was, *Stop fannying around and enjoy the music!* That certainly stopped me in my tracks after all the channelling I'd attempted. It wasn't what you'd think you might hear coming from a higher being. After all my own self-doubt, worrying if it was just my own mind creating these words in my head, if there was one thing I would not have expected to hear then it would be that. And I never use the word 'fanny'! All I could do was burst out laughing. It was a beautiful moment of confirmation for me.

The messenger told me that they, the higher council, were okaying my harp purchase and confirming that I would find one that day. They then went on to offer me many beautiful pieces of guidance.

It was getting on for half past five now and I had a feeling all the information had been imparted to me.

I had been busy trying to scribble key points down when the messenger said, "Oh yes, about the *Shrek* thing..." Well, I had to admit that had happened almost an hour before and I'd completely forgotten about it. Again, another reminder that I wasn't making all this up. He went on to explain that this higher being is 'beyond beauty' as I could understand it, beyond third-dimensional comprehension of beauty. She is pure vibration, not human, so she came to me in the best guise she could that I could conceive: a beautiful Greek goddess. However, this human state, however beautiful it might seem to me, diminishes her actual beauty to such an extent, it would be the same as a Greek goddess turning herself into an ogre. I had to admit I was completely bowled over by this; it was such a mind-blowing concept and put across to me in such a simple, cartoon image. It felt like, with their vast knowledge, they were imparting a little pearl, a little taster to me in a form that was beautifully childlike so I could fully grasp it. Although it seemed like they were just playing with me, it wasn't given in a condescending manner, far from it. Any more information would have fried my little brain. As it is I still shake my head in disbelief when I tell this story... and I do love telling it.

It wasn't over yet; just when I thought I'd had all I could handle for one night something extraordinary happened. The only way I can explain it is to say it was as if I was picked up and thrown into the sunrise. Feeling like I was being immersed in the clear blue-white of the morning sky, I believed I was being given a timeless quantum moment where I could experience the fifth dimension. It was bliss beyond words, beyond anything I've ever experienced and I can only compare it to other people's experiences of near-death, except I did not have to live through any of the traumas of actually nearly dying. I know I will never stop being grateful for this as long as I live, and as I explained in Scorpio it was this that helped me handle the death of my friend Rich and I hope will continue to help me with other losses I will have to experience in the future.

As I returned from this other world, all I could do was cry. It wasn't the normal tears I've shed, sobs that you hold in and that make you shake with the tension you carry. It was a release in the most exultant sense of the word, with the tears of joy flowing out of me like a river. If you've been there, you'll know what I mean.

This experience and these images have stayed clear in my

mind for all this time and I never expected to understand it any more deeply than what I thought I had grasped in the year or so that followed. But of course, more was to come.

Grounding this energy was going to be an important task for me. I needed to integrate it in a way that made sense for me and would help me keep my feet fully rooted to the earth. As I kept myself open, the guidance kept flowing even if patience was needed.

Six years later, at the end of 2009 my class-teaching job in school drew to a close and it was due to finish on a real high. My last day was the school carol service in the local church where the whole school would be singing carols, part-songs and modern songs with three-part harmonies, all challenging in varying degrees when you remember these children were seven to eleven years old. I would be conducting the choir and orchestra and I must admit, when it came to the day, I was excited and a little apprehensive for myself rather than the children. It was a wonderful send-off for me and I was very proud of them. During the day one of the teachers had told me how the Year Three class had been drawing angels and that one girl drew an angel with black shoes. Another girl had piped up and said that angels couldn't possibly have black shoes. The teacher in her role as secular mentor had to be careful what she said, and told me that she had told the children that as we don't know what angels really look like, the child could draw whatever she believed they would look like and that was fine. Very diplomatic I thought, though I was questioning in my mind whether angels would have black shoes.

When I went to bed that night with my head full of carol services and angels with black shoes, I asked what it was all about. Although I know this method as a tried and tested way of getting answers, I surprised even myself with the clarity of the reply I received as I awoke. The answer was multi-levelled and pulled together many stories I had been holding on to for a while but as yet had not found the right glue.

When I first began working with sound healing, the first book I was given was called *Healing Sounds* by Jonathan Goldman. In his introduction he talks about going to hear a Sufi spiritual leader speak on the subject of healing with light and sound. At the end he managed to speak to the great man and asked him if there was a relationship between tones and chakras. The man agreed and said he thought there was. However, after some consideration he said that he believed that the true healing power of sound was to be found in harmonics.[2]

This is something I have been working with for years, yet the message I awoke with opened up a far deeper explanation. My mind was somehow aware that each tone or frequency in the harmonic series is a vibration that carries wisdom, knowledge and healing within it, and that each harmonic frequency is represented by an angelic realm manifested in light and sound. The understanding given to me was that as we encounter the angel, or vibration, the information we receive is translated into something we can understand and relate to, i.e. the human form, as part of the light frequency.

This is how we translate the information in our minds and because it is coming from a far higher realm this helps us feel comfortable with it. This vibration is no more human than God is but as we receive the energy, we make it our own and I feel that is right and good. These higher energies have the ability to shape-shift as they connect to each individual. This is why God, the vibration, has a different face for each culture in the world and I suppose in the universe too. It would serve us to recognise that we create the image of God, the 'all that is' life force, in our own image, as our own reflection, our father. As there are many cultures, so there are many images of God. Learning to tolerate our different views will only come when we learn to tolerate the differences in each other and see them as beautiful. As we learn to see them as the many expressions of God, then we will begin to remove the fear.

I then remembered the experience when I saw my higher self and how she turned herself into a *Shrek* ogre. What I was seeing were the many different versions of her as she shape-shifted, translating her energy from the information held in her vibration; each vision a profound and sometimes humorous lesson.

But what of the black shoes? It just so happened that at that time I had just ordered a book online, recommended by John Wadsworth, called *Harmonies of Heaven and Earth* by Joscelyn Godwin; I thought I might find the answer there. He offered many interesting insights. Within the harmonic range of any note, the whole spectrum contains many combinations of sounds, which could be related to all kinds of physical states of being. There is a triad: three notes that sound in harmony to each other. These can be seen as the trinity, the higher states of being as in the I Ching masculine 'all that is' energy. It is represented numerically as three and the sound is harmonious. There are many combinations of notes offering the duality of two, the feminine receptive energy, which could be harmonious or discordant. And there is the diminished fifth, also known as a tritone.

When I went to various musical dictionaries to discover its history, the first piece of information I found called this interval the *Diabolus in musica*, the devil in music. But I was also aware that Berendt spoke of Schubert calling this a 'green' interval, and scientists were now discovering a connection of this tritone with photosynthesis.

It seemed there were going to be no straightforward answers, no black or white. The more I investigated the more I felt there was to research, and the more I found that different people were finding their own similar but slightly varied answers. I decided to release the whole process back into the ocean, like a fish I had caught but had no desire to eat. I sensed that the variety of vibrational sounds, from the subsonic to the ultrasonic, were all around us and we can choose to tune into them in many ways. Whether we see angels, black shoes on angels, devils or hear a resonance, how it manifests itself to us is also dependant on the vibration of our energy field at the time. How we interpret it is up to us as, I have said, we are the participant, not just the observer. As the frequency waves unlock the door to our emotions, we can use the higher frequencies to lift ourselves out of the lower vibrations of fear and the limitations of the ego, into the vibration and realms of love.

The more I look at this, the more I see how we can change the preconceptions we've built into our society if we can just take a new look at our view of the universe. For me this all starts by working with the healing of our voice, the manifestation of our own personal vibration. As I begin to understand just how powerful it is and how the absence of this tool in our lives leads to so much dis-ease I feel I am attracting people into my world that continually flag this up. So many people tell me how they never sing, or how they hate their voice. One of the saddest stories I heard was when a woman told me how she was forbidden to sing as a child and another who had to 'sing in secret'.

So many children have been told how awful their voices are when they first start to sing, it closes them down completely. This can lead to so many problems in later life, which are rarely traced back to this early abuse. There are also many people who simply judge their voices so harshly that they never bring singing into their lives at all. I explain to them that we all sing, just like we all breathe and walk and talk. If you've had an accident and have bit of a limp you don't stop walking because you don't walk perfectly anymore. Everyone's vibration is important; everyone's vibration has a part to play and makes up part of the whole vibration that makes up humanity. It is not to be denied. We must stop judging each other, and even more importantly we must stop judging ourselves.

There is a beautiful old story about a woman who has to carry a yoke on her shoulders with two buckets of water up from the river each day. It is a long trek down the hill and back up with the heavy buckets and the bucket that is attached to the left-hand side of her yoke has a crack in it. Each day she curses the broken bucket, as it always is half-empty by the time she arrives back to her house. As the weeks progress she is slowly made aware of the beautiful flowers that have grown up on her left as she walks back up the hill and it soon begins to dawn on her that it is the broken bucket that is allowing water to spill on to the path which has brought about this beautiful feast for her eyes to brighten up her journey.

We are all broken buckets in some ways, but that must not stop us from singing it out strong. In fact there's all the more reason, for in singing out we heal ourselves. We all have something to offer and a part to play and I do feel our judgement has become our obstacle. Although there is nothing wrong with striving for perfection, we must learn to accept everyone on their journey and remember that even if someone sings 'out of tune' they might be adding an important reflection and balance to what is needed. However, my work so far has brought me to believe that even being 'tone-deaf' is mostly created by judgement and can be healed.

As I begin to draw this book to a close I realise that there is always new information waiting around the corner, which makes it extremely difficult to be able to reach any point of conclusion. The invitations to continue on our path are always there if we are open to them.

In 2011, my good friend Seb bought me a beautiful crystal,

a green moldavite pendant as a thank-you for supporting her through a tough 2010. This crystal is a piece of meteorite, heaven brought down to Earth – it has a powerful energy. Some find it too difficult to wear for long periods of time. I, however, don't seem to be able to take it off.

As she gave it to me she held it up to the light and said, "If you look closely you can see Mary holding the baby Jesus." It has taken me many years to feel comfortable with the story of Jesus but with my journey has come an understanding of all the prophets and what their individual stories have offered us. It is my belief that Jesus brought a very powerful resonance to Earth and here I was being gifted with a beautiful reminder of that. She gave it to me on a Thursday and by Saturday all manner of things started to manifest themselves. It began with two fairly insignificant incidences that seemed to collide.

A few weeks before I received the crystal, Tareth invited me to another of his sound transmissions where he would be manifesting sound from a crystal, and this was being offered only to a small group of people on the Sunday afternoon, three days after I received Seb's gift. Still capable of blocking my flow of money into my life I wrote back thanking him for the invite but saying I didn't have the money at the time, even though it was only about £35. By the Saturday morning, he had got back to me and said there was a space for me and I could offer whatever I could afford. This wasn't the first time this had happened and I understood that I was being offered the place for a reason even if I didn't know what it was yet. I had to remind myself that every time I stepped, or prepared to step, into the Glastonbury Zodiac, magic would start to happen.

Around the same time, I reconnected with my old crystal healer, John, who helped me with my past life regression, and whom I hadn't seen for a few years. Whilst on the phone to

him and having told him about my voice work, he said he was
getting some guidance for me.

The guidance explained how, in a past life, I had closed
down my connection to the Christ consciousness. This is,
of course, a universal story, but I was at a point in my life
when I needed to hear it again. He then gave me a procedure,
explaining that as my heart chakra was still closed on some
level, I should demand that the golden key to my heart be
returned to me so I could open that door again.

At that point I laughed. "John," I said, "did you know the
name of my project is *Keys to the Golden City*?"

It was as though a huge chime of recognition was
sounding inside of me. I told him I would do the procedure
but as I now knew why I was being offered the place at
Tareth's healing session I said I would wait till after I'd
received the necessary transmissions.

As I arrived at Tareth's door I was holding back the tears as
the full force of the significance of my story was beginning to
dawn on me. I was realising that I had failed to use my voice
many times, including in my Tudor past life as I chose to die
rather than face my pain. I was beginning to understand that in
this present life I was being gifted the chance to rediscover my
voice and unlock the door to my golden city. Now the universe
was working with me on this. Tareth only invited twelve people
to his transmissions that day and the fact that there was a space
for me was leaving me speechless and very tearful.

He also suggested we brought a crystal of our own to
energise with the sounds he was bringing through. I always
used a large amethyst for my healings so I brought this one.
It works for the crown chakra so I thought it would be good
for my Pisces and higher chakra energy. As Tareth's crystal
began singing so beautifully the tears flowed freely down my
cheeks, but then suddenly I realised my error. I had brought
a crown chakra crystal to the session, but it was my desire to

heal my heart chakra. I should have brought a green or a rose quartz. I began tutting to myself under my breath for being so thoughtless and was trying to think of a way to solve this – maybe I had a rose quartz in my bag I could ask Tareth to sound into again. As I felt my brain getting busy I knew I was losing the beautiful energy I was being gifted when suddenly my hand reached for the green moldavite hanging around my neck just at my heart chakra. Now the tears were unstoppable as I realised Seb's crystal was there all the time, not only helping to bring this healing into being but playing a starring role in just being; a lesson I dearly need to remember and stop giving myself an unnecessarily hard time. Everything had already been put in place, I just needed to relax and offer my gratitude. I could do nothing but sob.

At the end of the session we each had a one-to-one with Tareth. I naturally mentioned the procedure I wanted to work through after leaving this healing session. Tareth very clearly saw that I would be successful in stepping into my heart, but he added that I shouldn't 'look back'. Not understanding fully what this meant I returned and went through the procedure John had explained to me. It all went well except that when I had the key in my hand and opened the big gates I had trouble keeping them open. I could see this was going to take a little more work.

A few weeks later I attended John Wadsworth's Pisces day, my third visit to his Pisces workshop, and he asked me to accompany his meditation with my harp, which of course I was more than happy to do. The meditation was based on the story of *Orpheus and the Underworld*. After losing his beloved wife, he journeys to find her in the underworld and asks Hades, or Pluto, god of the underworld, for her to be returned to him. He wins Hades over with his beautiful harp-playing. Orpheus is told he can have his wife back as long as when she follows behind him he doesn't turn around to look at her until they are safely out of the underworld. Orpheus of course agrees but cannot contain himself, and looks back just when he nearly has her within his reach. It is a tragic story as she is then lost to him forever. When asked about our comments on the meditation I just felt it was speaking directly to me. This was now the second time I had been told not to look back.

That night, after watching the four-hour DVD of the Henry VIII story and then throwing up violently at four in the morning, I finally took heed. It was time for me to stop looking back into my past lives; they had served their purpose. I now needed to step forward into the new phase of my life.

With the months that passed, I realised that I had unconsciously been living very astrologically, inspired, of course, by John Wadsworth's Alchemical Journey. As I locked into the enriching archetypal energy of each month and the lessons I could learn from each, by Pisces, I had received a wonderful healing mechanism called the Sedona Method, a ten-CD process of letting go. For me it was gentle yet powerful. In Aries, I began to learn to live alone happily and by Taurus felt fully in my abundance, happy in the knowledge that all I needed was here inside me. I'd found my story, who I am and why I'm here. Even if that story is simply to be; to be happy. I know that this is a blessed state to live in and it wasn't long before people started asking me if I'd met someone.

"You look as if you're in love," friends were saying. I just replied that I was at last in love with myself. What a perfect place to start the rest of your life from.

In Gemini 2011 I began the rewrite of this book, looking to tie the loose threads together. To finish my Libra story, Louise brought me back on track with my connection to the Christ consciousness. As I revisited my journey in Scorpio, of breaking the pact that was stopping me from entering my golden city, I realised, two years on, this had totally slipped my mind. Recalling the sequence of synchronicities that brought me to this position, closer to my heart than I could ever have imagined, I could only chuckle. I reminded myself that we can get a far better sense of flow when our eye is off the ball.

As the autumn set in, my asthma gently returned to me. I realised that although I had peeled back a good few layers, I hadn't reached the deepest aspect of the healing needed. I had completed the journey to my golden city and retrieved the key, however, even though I was at the threshold, with all this in place, I still wasn't ready to turn the key and step in. I had to admit I felt a good deal of disappointment on many levels, but I recognised that life is long and there would be many more stories and opportunities to come. That is what makes our journey interesting; the rich tapestry of life. I had only been on this healing path for just over twelve years; I was only a beginner, even though I knew I had been travelling on it subconsciously all my life. The need to heal the asthma I was still holding in my body, was going to take several more years to complete. Luckily I have never had a problem with time.

Looking back I now understood why at fourteen I had joined my Baptist church youth group, somehow recognising my call back to the Christ consciousness. However, in this life, at fourteen, I was too closed to pick up the breadcrumbs I had left. Both the story told to me by the Baptists of the marriage in heaven, and the story of our planets' shift in the solar system told to me by the woman in Hong Kong, were stories of ascension. But I was only now realising they were stories that were offering personal guidance to me. I needed to step inside the gates to my golden city, so I could receive the Christ consciousness vibration and open my heart completely. It was the moldavite crystal that was manifesting this understanding for me with such clarity, beautifully showing the concept of the meteorite bringing heaven to Earth.

I had been holding on to an idea that the first twelve harmonics related to the twelve angelic realms and that once you embody all those energies completely you can access and step into the Christ consciousness, the thirteenth ray. This vibration was the energy that Jesus embodied, and that's why he was called Christ. He was, of course, a Christ, a man able to bring that energy to Earth.

This twelve-month process, travelling around the year, is just one of many mirrors but the tools offer a beautiful way to integrate all the aspects of ourselves into a feeling of harmony. As we turn the wheel through the year we arrive at the last stage in a state of grace, becoming the elders of our community, revered and respected members of a people who understand why we are here and what our role in life is. Embracing this journey invites us all to embody this way of being, this higher vibration; the thirteenth ray.

As we are all walking this road together, we are going to form a bride for God. The masculine, Creative Heaven and we, the feminine, the Receptive Earth, will marry and find a state of balance. This will be experienced inside ourselves. This concept of balance within each of us will bring about the marriage of our personal idea of duality. We can all open the gates to our golden city as one. (This is just a human view of the transition, of course. God, being the highest vibration, is whole and needs no bride. It's not even right to say God is the bride and the groom because that creates a state of duality; God just is. This is just our way of creating a story we can relate to.)

The one thing I have always hoped to achieve in my life is to try and inspire others with what I do, and I know I am one of many. The vibration that we can put out needs to be supported by our positivity and strength of belief. If our chance to create this new way of being is on its way, but hangs in the balance because of our faith that it can happen, then there's only one thing we can do. We have to live as if it's already here. We have to remove all doubt so that those around us feel it too as we shine that Leo energy out. The individual becoming whole can then step into the Aquarian group.

As I know I'm not alone I know that this is happening all around the world, gradually inspiring and filling more and more with the hope and knowledge that it's up to us to step into a new world of our dreams. Together, we are creating a world of openness and fairness; a world where everyone is loved and treated with respect and feels a part of the community. Sensing that it's our role to bring this heavenly place to Earth is something I hope we can all see as part of our story, living it with every ounce of our being.

I knew that all these words I was writing suddenly had no real meaning. They are all just my conscious mind trying – there's that word 'trying' again – to work it all out. Busy, busy, busy. Where was the stillness? There was only one thing left to do: switch off the computer and allow you to discover your own story. I just need to sound my inner vibration, bringing it into manifestation as a process of learning to love myself ever more deeply as I arrive at the gates of my golden city, slip into the watery ocean of the oneness and just be.

I'd love to hear from you!

If you would like to discuss any of the matters in the book, keep in touch about Books 2 and 3 in the trilogy, or wish to find out more about my other work – performances, journeys, meditations or workshops – please visit www.keystothegoldencity.com

You can also follow me on Facebook, SoundCloud, Twitter or my Blogspot: Journey to the Golden City.

End Notes

Introduction

1. On the dodecahedron. In Plato's dialogue *Timaeus* (c. 360 BC) he says that apart from the four platonic solids present in the universe, *there is a fifth figure (which is made out of twelve pentagons), the dodecahedron – this God used as a model for the twelvefold division of the Zodiac.* (Plato, *Timaeus*, Jowett translation.) Another universal 'shape' put forward by scientists is the ring doughnut. I will look at this in a future publication. On researching my point about dodecahedrons in Wikipedia I had a little trouble finding the source of the quote. Eventually all I came across was an email address. Feeling I had no other option and expecting little, I didn't hold out much hope when I pressed send. However, I was in luck and not only did I get a response, but a lovely dialogue ensued. His name and email gave nothing away to start with so I had to be bold and ask where he was based. It turned out Magnus Wenninger was a leading researcher in an American university. His interest in my book was very flattering, and he was particularly interested in my desire to bring together the worlds of science and spirituality. It took a few emails

before he suggested I visited his website, and when I did I was amazed. I discovered he was also a Catholic priest. Of all the scientists I could have connected with, I picked one who was marrying these worlds perfectly. Further information can be sourced from www.saintjohnsabbey. org/wenninger.

2. On the musical cycle of fourths. I learned in my study of jazz that every musical ending, called a cadence, is usually made up of three chords, and in the 'perfect' ending or cadence the chords are all at an interval of a fourth from each other. The cycle of fourths travels through all twelve perfect cadences. Even before I developed this astrological view of the universe with the image of the Russian dolls and the dodecahedron, I saw how the journey around the musical cycle of fourths was a wheel that contained cycles within cycles. Each set of three chords is an ending, but continuously flows into the next cadence. Each chord is a beginning, a middle and an end. It is always beginning, always ending and always moving. It is a perfect reflection of all that is.

3. On investigation I discovered that a rhombic dodecahedron is not only one of the few shapes that can be used to fill three-dimensional space, perfectly without any gaps, but of these shapes, it has the most sides possible for tessellation to work.

4. A. T. Mann has written many books on astrology, *derived from the work of G. I. Gurdjieff, P. D. Ouspensky and Rodney Collin,* based on the idea that it relates to time in an incremental or logarithmic way, calling it Life Time Astrology. Mann has mapped the seasonal, astrological year alongside the journey of the human lifetime in the way of the twelve ages of man.

Chapter 2

1. Actually this chubby Buddha isn't Buddha at all. He is Ho-tei, a Chinese Taoist monk, possessed of all vices, but a lover of fun. He is a traditional figure in Chinese religion, representing what you could call the Taurus side of life. In Western society Ho-tei has been widely misinterpreted as a figure of Buddha. (Johanna van Fessem.)
2. D. Chopra. *Ageless Body, Timeless Mind*, p. 188.
3. P. Coelho. *The Valkyries*, p. 199.

Chapter 5

1. Music that formed in the West is mostly based on major and minor scales or keys. I have always understood these to be, respectively, masculine and feminine in quality. This became ever more evident as I began working with sound healing.
2. The amazing phenomena of the Glastonbury Zodiac and many others that have been discovered work with the idea that the star constellations are reflected and can be mapped out in our landscape as massive effigies. These are outlined by features such as rivers and woods, paths, tracks and field boundaries.
3. *"Our deepest fear is not that we are inadequate. Our deepest fear is that we are powerful beyond measure. It is our light, not our darkness that most frightens us... And as we let our own light shine, we unconsciously give other people permission to do the same."* Marianne Williamson, *A Return to Love: Reflections on the Principles of a Course in Miracles*, p. 190–91.
4. *The Fellowship of the Ring*. Director: Peter Jackson. Wingnut Films, the Saul Zaentz Company, 2001.
5. Bill Bryson, *A Short History of Nearly Everything*, p. 161.

N.B. *10^{18} joules of potential energy* means 10 to the power of 18 i.e. 10 with 18 zeros after it.

Chapter 7

1. It is interesting to note that, in music, the intervals of a 4th, 5th (and the octave) are called 'perfect' where all the others are all called major or minor. A perfect 4th is the mirror of the perfect 5th because the same notes are used, i.e. C to F is a 4th and F to C is a 5th.

The Golden Mirror

I spent my life looking in the mirror waiting for you to make a move
And all you do is stare right back at me.
What could I do when I thought my ball was in the other court
And all you do is throw it back at me?

I wanted to scream, shout and rail and smash it to the floor
But then I knew that would never settle the score.

Now look at me,
I'm standing here caught between the smile and the pout.
And all you do is turn your back on me.
Now I have heard if we don't go within then we go without.
Now I'm alone I'm missing you strongly.

I close my eyes hoping I would find another way
And in the dark your light shone brighter than the day

Hold on. I'm not one to get sold on new ways of living
But if you can show me how I can
Break through my doubts and misgivings.

Then you say, don't believe that all you see is true
All that you see is just a reflection of you.

Hold on. It's gonna be a journey of golden ways of living
If you can see through this illusion you'll find new
Ways of forgiving
Look through this two-way mirror and see you and me as
one.
If you can break through this illusion
It frees you into the one.

See yourself and all the golden love that we can share
Tell yourself these fears we can repair, tell yourself
I love you, please forgive me, thank you
I love you, I'm sorry, please forgive, thank you
I love you.

Chapter 8

1. Taken from the *Gospel of Thomas*, a list of one hundred say-
   ings that Jesus spoke (No. 70).

Chapter 9

1. Robert Pirsig, *Zen and the Art of Motorcycle Maintenance*, p.
   134.

Chapter 11

1. Equal temperament is a system of tuning that tunes all adjacent notes to an exact frequency ratio to each other, removing the slight differences that naturally occur.
2. Stephen Hawking, *A Brief History of Time*, p. 122.
3. Ibid., p.165.
4. Hawking, op. cit., p.174.
5. Schrödinger's cat is a paradoxical experiment devised by the Austrian physicist Erwin Schrodinger in 1935. It offers the idea that a cat, whilst hidden inside a box, can be either alive or dead, depending on what has occured inside. The answer is only known when the box is opened and the observer brings one of the possibilities into play, simply by witnessing it. Before this, both states are possible.

Chapter 12

1. Ernst Berendt, *The World Is Sound: Nada Brahma*, p. 68.
2. Jonathan Goldman, *Healing Sounds*, p. 2.

Bibliography

Berendt, Joachim-Ernst. *The World Is Sound: Nada Brahma.* Rochester Vermont: Destiny Book, a division of Inner Traditions International, 1983 (English translation 1987).

Berendt, Joachim-Ernst. *The Third Ear: On Listening to the World.* London: HarperCollins, 1988.

Bettelheim, Bruno. *Uses of Enchantment.* London: Penguin Books Ltd, 1991.

Brown, Dan. *The Da Vinci Code.* London: Bantam Press, imprint of Transworld Publishers Ltd, 2003.

Bryson, Bill. *A Short History of Nearly Everything.* London: Doubleday, a division of Transworld Publishers Ltd, 2003.

Chopra, Deepak. *SynchroDestiny.* London: Random House, 2003.

Coelho, Paulo. *The Alchemist.* London: HarperCollins Publishers, 1998.

Coelho, Paulo. *The Valkyries.* London: HarperCollins Publishers, 1998.

Divine, John the. *The Revelation, From the Authorized King James Version of the New Testament.* New York: Oxford University Press, 1997.

Godwin, Joscelyn. *Harmonies of Heaven and Earth.* Rochester Vermont: Inner Traditions International, 1987.

Goldman, Jonathan. *Healing Sounds: The Power of Harmonics*. Shaftesbury, UK: Element Books Ltd, 1992.

Hawking, Stephen W. *A Brief History of Time: From the Big Bang to Black Holes*. London: Transworld Publishers Ltd, 1988.

Keenan, Brian. *Turlough*. London: Vintage Publishing imprint of Random House, 2001.

Mann, A. T. *The Divine Life: Astrology and Reincarnation*. Shaftesbury, UK: Element Books Ltd, 1984.

Paul, Haydn. *Revolutionary Spirit: Exploring the Astrological Uranus*. London: HarperCollins, 1992.

Philp, Chrissy. *The Golden City: Reality Model for a New Age, Book 2*. Self-published, 1996.

Pirsig, Robert. *Zen and the Art of Motorcycle Maintenance*. London: Transworld Publishers Ltd, 1974.

Redfield, James. *The Celestine Prophecy*. London: Transworld Publishers, Random House, 1991.

Robbins, Tom. *Jitterbug Perfume*. New York: Bantam Books, Random House, 1984.

Leitch, Yuri (editor). *Signs & Secrets of the Glastonbury Zodiac: The Maltwood Moot Anthology, Vol. I*. Glastonbury: Archive Publishing, 2012.

Thomas. *Gospel of Thomas, From the Authorized King James Version of the New Testament*. New York: Oxford University Press, 1997.

Tolle, Eckhart. *A New Earth*. London: Penguin Books Ltd, 2005.

Trismegistus, Hermes. *The Hermetica*. Whitefish USA: R. A. Kessinger, 1998.

Vitale, Joe. *Zero Limits*. Chichester: John Wiley & Sons Ltd, 2007.

Walsch, Neale Donald. *Communion with God*. California: Mobius, 2000.

Wilhelm, Richard (translator). *I Ching*. London: Penguin Books Ltd, 1968.

Williamson, Marianne. A *Return to Love: Reflections on the Principles of a Course in Miracles*. London: HarperCollins, 1992.

Discography

Bach, J. S. *The Well-Tempered Clavier*. California: Alfred Music Publishing (since 1922).

Goodchild, Chloe. *Your Naked Voice*. Three CDS available from www.thenakedvoice.com.

Holst, Gustav. *The Planets*. London: Boosey & Hawkes (since 1930).

Purce, Jill. *The Healing Voice*. CD available from www.jillpurce.com.

Further Reference

John Wadsworth: www.thealchemicaljourney.co.uk

Chloe Goodchild: www.thenakedvoice.com

A. T. Mann: www.atmann.net

Tareth: www.tareth.co.uk

Magnus Wenninger: visit his Wikipedia page to find more info and links to his website.

The Sedona Method: www.sedona.com